Pinch OF Nom

BUDGET

First published 2023 by Bluebird
an imprint of Pan Macmillan
The Smithson, 6 Briset Street, London EC1M 5NR
EU representative: Macmillan Publishers Ireland Ltd, 1st Floor,
The Liffey Trust Centre, 117–126 Sheriff Street Upper,
Dublin 1, D01 YC43

Associated companies throughout the world
www.panmacmillan.com

ISBN 978-1-0350-2217-5

1 3 5 7 9 8 6 4 2
A CIP catalogue record for this book is available from the British Library.
Printed and bound in China.

Publisher Carole Tonkinson
Managing Editor Martha Burley
Production Manager Alenka Oblak
Art Direction and Design Studio Nic&Lou
Illustrations Beth Free / Shutterstock
Food Styling Kate Wesson and Octavia Squire
Prop Styling Max Robinson

Visit www.panmacmillan.com to read more about all our books
and to buy them. You will also find features, author interviews and
news of any author events, and you can sign up for e-newsletters
so that you're always first to hear about our new releases.

Kate & Kay Allinson

Pinch OF Nom BUDGET

AFFORDABLE, DELICIOUS FOOD

bluebird
books for life

CONTENTS

HELLO *and* WELCOME

Here we are sharing a brand-new cookbook with you! Whether you're new to Pinch of Nom, or you've followed our journey from the start, it's a privilege to be bringing you another book full of tasty, slimming-friendly recipes. It's impossible to ignore that costs are on the rise, and we know it's more important than ever that the food you put on the table works for your budget. While we've always prioritized using inexpensive ingredients that stretch across multiple meals, the recipes in this book go a step further to put value first. Eating healthy, delicious food shouldn't be a luxury, and that's why Budget is chock-full of pocket-friendly mains and desserts that bring all the flavour, for a fraction of the cost.

NEW LOOK, SAME US

This paperback is a fresh look for us, bringing you a selection of recipes on a more specific theme than our bigger, hardback cookbooks. Where the hardbacks are brimming with flavour-packed dishes for different occasions, we've narrowed down the 75 recipes in this book to only those that fit our *Budget* theme.

We've stuck to two chapters: mains and desserts. We know these are the pages you turn to time and time again. So we've brought you 55 main courses that you can rustle up for lunch or dinner, and 20 desserts for when you fancy something sweet. It might be a new format, but it's all the same Pinch of Nom flavour that you know and love.

SO, WHY BUDGET?

You can't beat the happiness that a nourishing, home-cooked meal brings. By reinventing old favourites, trying classic flavours in new ways and making the most of our store cupboard, we've managed to put together our most affordable collection of recipes yet. Cutting the cost of our ingredients lists and scaling back on non-essentials means we've got your budget in hand, without asking you to compromise on what you really want to eat.

There's nothing like the comfort of a familiar crowd-pleaser, and Pinch of Nom fans are sure to recognize a handful of the penny-friendly recipes we've included from the website. There are also plenty of dishes you've never seen before, including Mushroom Masala (page 66) and zingy Pineapple Pork (page 130).

Plus, you can rest assured that we've included everyone's favourite night of the week: Fakeaways! Trust us, you haven't lived until you've tried our Loaded Curry Burger (page 28). Piled high with Indian-inspired flavours, it gives you the best of two delicious worlds, without breaking the bank.

Feeling the squeeze? Don't forget to freeze! Batch-cooking makes it so much easier to put midweek favourites on the table night after night. You'll find our top batch-cooking hints and tips to help you along on pages 12–13.

These are ALL dinners and desserts you can rely on, even when you're feeling the pinch. We hope that this book helps to make life a bit easier for you, with recipes that you look forward to eating. Are you ready to tuck in?

Kay x *Kate*

THE FOOD

As a classically trained chef, Kate has always loved recreating dishes and putting an original spin on classic recipes. This is how the very first Pinch of Nom recipes came to be, and it's this passion that means we can continue to bring fresh new flavours to you today. Kate and her small team love nothing more than getting into the kitchen and experimenting with ingredients until some Pinch of Nom magic is created!

With all of our recipes, and especially the ones in this book, it's so important to us that we only ever use budget-friendly ingredients that can stretch across multiple dishes. Turning to store-cupboard staples and thrifty swaps, we've created new recipes that bring you value for money, as well as giving a few favourites a little budget makeover. You'll find some classic recipes from our website in this book, along with others that have been tweaked to streamline the ingredients list.

We've said goodbye to any expensive ingredients that you won't use often, and cut out any garnishes where the extra flavour doesn't outweigh the additional cost. If you've cooked from any of our previous books, you'll know we're all about flexible methods, so if something can be cooked in more than one way, we'll give you all the options. As always, the recipes are designed to suit any level of cooking skill, so even beginners can get stuck in!

Overall, the focus of this book is all about great-tasting food that won't break the bank. We aim to create recipes that everyone will enjoy, so keep an eye out for where we've flagged vegetarian, gluten-free or dairy-free recipes.

If you're watching the pennies, look out for the Super Saver flash icon on pages where the recipe offers especially good value for money.

RECIPE TAGS

EVERYDAY LIGHT

These recipes can be used freely throughout the week. All the meals, including accompaniments, are under 400 calories. Or, in the case of sweet treats, under 200 calories. Of course, if you're counting calories, you still need to keep an eye on the values, but these recipes should help you stay under your allowance.

WEEKLY INDULGENCE

These recipes are still low in calories (400–500 calories or 200–300 for sweet treats) but should be saved for once or twice a week. Mix them up with your Everyday Light recipes for variety.

SPECIAL OCCASION

These recipes are often lower in calories than their full-fat counterparts, but they need to be saved for a special occasion. This tag indicates any main meals that are over 500 calories, or over 300 for sweet treats.

KCAL and CARB VALUES*

All of our recipes have been worked out as complete meals, using standardized portion sizes for any accompaniments, as advised by the British Nutrition Foundation. Carb values are included for those who need to measure their intake.

GLUTEN-FREE RECIPES

We have marked gluten-free recipes with an icon. All these recipes are either free of gluten or we have suggested gluten-free ingredient swaps of common ingredients, such as stock cubes and Worcestershire sauce. Please check labelling to ensure the product you buy is gluten free.

FREEZABLE RECIPES

Look out for the 'Freeze Me' icon to indicate freezer-friendly dishes. The icon applies to the main dish only, not the suggested accompaniments.

SUPER SAVER FLASH

Brand new for this book, this handy sticker lets you know when a recipe is especially good value for money. These budget-friendly recipes are perfect for thrifty midweek meals, using inexpensive ingredients and store-cupboard staples.

OUR RECIPE ICONS

VEGGIE   FREEZE ME   DAIRY FREE   GLUTEN FREE

VEGAN   BATCH FRIENDLY   LOW CARB

All of these calculations and dietary indicators are for guidance only and are not to be taken as complete fact without checking ingredients and product labelling yourself.

BATCH COOKING

It's no secret that we love a good batch-cooking session. Batch cooking is all about getting the most from your ingredients, saving time and money. Stretch your food further by making bigger portions and bulking them out with vegetables that need using up. Most of the recipes you'll find in this book are freezer-friendly, so you can double up portions and enjoy your extras on another day. Our recipes come with specific refrigerating and freezing instructions to help you along, and we've included the latest NHS food-safety guidelines (correct at the time of writing). The definition of a 'batch-cook dream', our Mix-It-Up Mince (page 144) stretches into a whopping eight portions! It can be served with a variety of accompaniments, from your favourite kind of potatoes to fluffy rice – so you never feel like you're eating the same thing twice!

MAKE ROOM FOR LEFTOVERS

It's a good idea to check you've got space in your fridge or freezer before you start cooking. You don't want leftovers going to waste!

DIVIDE PORTIONS UP

No-one has time to chisel away at a huge, frozen block of food. Store leftovers in the fridge or freezer as individual-sized portions – your food will cool, freeze and defrost loads quicker.

USE AIRTIGHT CONTAINERS *and* FREEZER BAGS

Freezer-proof containers and bags don't have to be expensive. Containers that are also microwave-safe are the best investment, as there's no need to buy separate Tupperware for the sake of reheating. Whether you use containers or bags, make sure they seal properly to avoid 'freezer burn' (uninvited air damaging your food).

USE REFRIGERATED FOODS WITHIN 2–3 DAYS

Many recipes like curries and chilies taste even better after 24 hours in the fridge, but be mindful of how long you keep cooked food in the fridge. Cooked meals can be kept in the fridge for 2–3 days before there is a risk of food poisoning, so make sure to freeze meals straight away if you plan to eat them after this time.

PUT A LABEL ON IT

Extra portions can be stored away for busier days, but be sure to write the date you made it (and what it is!) on a freezer-proof sticker. Meals can be frozen for 3–6 months. Beyond

6 months is still safe, but the food may not taste as good.

ONLY REHEAT FOOD ONCE

See NHS guidelines (correct at the time of writing) below.

DEFROST THOROUGHLY

Don't reheat food until it has defrosted thoroughly in the fridge or microwave.

REHEAT *and* EAT WITHIN 24 HOURS

NHS guidelines (correct at the time of writing) state that you should reheat food until it reaches 70°C/158°F and holds that temperature for 2 minutes. Make sure it's piping hot throughout. Stir while reheating.

RICE *and* PASTA ARE BEST COOKED FRESH

You can freeze the sauce or meat for some recipes, but in most cases it'll be best to cook the accompaniments right before serving. Some foods can't be reheated or just taste a lot nicer when they're freshly cooked.

STORING RICE

Rice is safe to freeze and reheat, but only if it's stored in the right way. Cool it as quickly as possible (ideally within 1 hour) by putting it in a wide, shallow container. The longer rice is left at room temperature, the greater the risk that it could grow harmful bacteria. Keep cooked rice in the fridge no longer than 1 day before reheating it, or you can freeze it and defrost thoroughly in the fridge before reheating.

Always make sure you reheat rice until it is piping hot, and **never** reheat it more than once.

KEY INGREDIENTS

STORE CUPBOARD

Keep an eye out for the 'SC' badge on the ingredients on the next few pages. We've given store-cupboard ingredients this special marker. They're staples you can keep in the cupboard and use time and again before needing to replenish them. Using store-cupboard ingredients can really cut down your costs, rather than buying individual items for a recipe.

PROTEIN

While we were putting the recipes for this book together, we were conscious of using meats from the more affordable end of the scale (cuts of beef, for example, are usually pricier than chicken!). In many of our recipes you'll find that you can switch the type of protein for any meat that suits your budget better. This especially applies to any mince recipes; turkey, beef or pork mince are easily interchangeable. In all cases where meat is used in this book, we'd recommend using the leanest possible cuts and trimming off all visible fat. Lean meats are a great source of protein, providing essential nutrients and keeping you feeling full between meals. And don't forget, vegetarian protein options can always be used instead of meat in all of the recipes in this book.

HERBS *and* SPICES SC

Herbs and spices keep your food interesting without the need to break the bank. We've used inexpensive dried ingredients where possible, with fresh ingredients only where they're necessary to get the flavour of a dish just right. Homemade spice blends and sauces

taste so much better than shop-bought versions, and you can put them together for a fraction of the cost. For our budget-friendly Mushroom Masala (page 66), we've blended veg with store-cupboard herbs and spices to make our aromatic sauce. Don't be shy with spices – not all of them burn your mouth off! We've added a spice-level icon to the recipes in this book, so you know what to expect. Always taste your food before adding extra spicing; this is particularly important if you're planning to double the quantities of sauce in a recipe. You'll often find that you don't need to double the amount of all the ingredients to achieve the right flavour – spices, vinegars, mustard and hot sauces should be added gradually, to taste.

STOCKS, SAUCE *and* THICKENERS SC

When you remove fat from a dish, flavours can dwindle. Adding spices is one way to boost flavours, but often the level of acidity in a recipe is much more important. When it comes to balancing and boosting flavours in our dishes, we love to use vinegar, soy sauce, Worcestershire sauce or Henderson's relish. One of Pinch of Nom's essential ingredients is the humble stock cube or stock pot; they add instant flavour and they're so versatile. We use various flavoured stock cubes and pots throughout this book, but there's always an option if you can't get your hands on the exact ones we've used. White wine stock pots, for example, can be tricky to find, but you can use 100ml of dry white wine and reduce the amount of water used in the recipe by 100ml instead (this will add extra calories). It's worth noting that sauces, stock cubes and pots are often high in salt, so you may want to swap for reduced-salt versions.

We're often asked for tips on how to thicken soups, sauces and gravies. In the pre-slimming days, we wouldn't have thought twice about using a few tablespoons of flour to thicken liquids. Nowadays we're always on the lookout for lower-calorie and gluten-free options. Letting liquids reduce is a good way of thickening sauces without adding anything extra. As the moisture evaporates, the flavours get more concentrated too, so the end result will taste even better.

You can also thicken recipes with potatoes (yes, really!). They're super starchy so they can be blitzed or mashed into your sauce or soup to soak up extra liquid. Bear in mind that this method will add some extra calories (1 large potato, approx. 369g, is about 311 kcal). A tomato-based dish such as tomato soup or bolognese can be thickened slightly using some tomato puree. This will add about 50 kcal per 51g tablespoon.

You can use egg yolks or whole beaten eggs to thicken some soups and sauces. Drizzle a little of the hot liquid onto the egg, whisking vigorously, then stir the egg into the pan and heat gently until it thickens. 1 medium (57g) egg is about 76 kcal and 1 medium (18g) egg yolk is about 55 kcal.

If making a roux-style sauce you can cut down on calories by making a slurry rather than using loads of butter. Simply mix your measured-out flour with a little water, then stir it into boiling liquid and simmer for a few minutes to cook the flour. 1 level tablespoon (20g) of plain flour is about 71 kcal. Another instant way to thicken any mixture is by using cornflour. This needs to be made into a slurry by adding a little cold water and then adding to the boiling liquid. Be sure to cook it until the starchy taste has gone. 1 level tablespoon of cornflour (20g) is about 69 kcal. It can be tempting to thicken stews or chillies with gravy granules, but this can add quite a few calories if you have a heavy hand. 1 teaspoon (5g) of gravy granules is about 21 kcal (depending on the brand). It's worth bearing in mind that gravy granules can also be high in salt.

LEMONS *and* LIMES

Fresh lemons and limes pack a punch when it comes to flavour. Using citrusy alternatives like lemon curd, bottled lemon and lime juice can be more cost effective – just be sure to refrigerate them once opened. Lemon curd adds a moreish tang to the light sponge in our Lemon Curd Swiss Roll on page 164.

REDUCED-FAT DAIRY

Substituting high-fat dairy products with clever alternatives can make a dish instantly lower in calories. You'll find that we'll often use reduced-fat cream cheese or spreadable cheese rather than the higher-fat versions. The same applies to any recipes that may traditionally contain heavy, high-calorie cream. We have swapped this out for a light double cream alternative such as Elmlea.

PLANT-BASED ALTERNATIVES

We often use plant-based alternatives to dairy milk because they're low in fat and add flavour to a dish. Coconut dairy-free milk alternative is a great substitute for high-fat tinned coconut milk, and almond milk adds a lovely nutty flavour when it's added into recipes. Make sure you pick up the unsweetened coconut or almond milk alternatives rather than any tinned versions; these will normally be found in a carton container.

TINS SC

Don't be afraid to bulk-buy tinned essentials! Beans, tomatoes, lentils, sweetcorn and tuna all come in handy time and time again. We often use them to add texture and flavour to stews, soups and salads. Using tinned ingredients can really help to keep costs down, and you'll never know the difference – used in these sorts of recipes they'll taste just as good as their fresh counterparts.

FROZEN FRUIT *and* VEG

Frozen fruit and veg make great filler ingredients and are perfect low-cost alternatives for recipes such as stews, where fresh ingredients aren't always necessary. Most of the time they're already peeled and chopped too, so they save time as well as money; you can just throw them in alongside your other ingredients.

PULSES *and* BEANS **SC**

High in both protein and fibre, keeping a few tins of beans and pulses in the cupboard is never going to do any harm! They're great for bulking out soups, stews, casseroles and curries.

PASTA *and* RICE **SC**

Pasta and rice are fantastic, budget-friendly fillers you can rely on to make so many Pinch of Nom recipes. From pasta bakes to one-pot rice dishes, you'll reach for these cupboard-friendly staples time and time again.

BREAD **SC**

A great source of fibre, wholemeal bread is filling and versatile too – you'll need some wholemeal rolls for our tasty Enchilada Sliders (page 114). We often use gluten-free breads as they tend to contain fewer calories and less sugar, making them an easy swap when you want to shave off a few calories.

EGGS **SC**

Eggs are protein-rich, tasty and versatile! The humble egg can be used in so many different ways. They're especially useful for baking as they're so good at binding ingredients together, and we couldn't make our irresistible Orange Ricotta Cake (page 161) without them.

LOW-CALORIE COOKING SPRAY **SC**

One of the best ways to cut down on cooking with oils and fats is to use a low-calorie cooking spray. A spritz of this will make little difference to the end result of your food, but it can make a huge difference to the calories consumed.

READY-MADE PASTRY

There's no need to become a pastry chef overnight – just buy it ready-made! Not only can you usually find a light version with reduced calories, it saves so much time and hassle when making our Tomato and Caramelized Onion Tarts (page 135).

TORTILLA WRAPS

Pinch of Nom is well known for creating magic with wraps! Wholegrain or wholewheat wraps provide fibre and fill you up too. You can use them to create our flavourful Veggie Quesadillas (page 61), using a handy hack to fold them into neat little triangles.

SWEETENER **SC**

There are so many sweeteners out there, it can be tricky to know which is the best substitute for regular sugar. Sweeteners vary in sweetness and swapping them weight-for-weight with regular sugar can give you different results. In our recipes we use granulated sweetener, not powdered sweetener, as it has larger 'crystals'. This can be used weight-for-weight anywhere that you're replacing sugar.

OUR FAVOURITE KIT

NON-STICK PANS

If there's one bit of kit that Pinch of Nom would advise as an investment kitchen piece, it would be a decent set of non-stick pans. The better the non-stick quality of your pans, the fewer cooking oils and fats you'll need to use in order to stop food sticking and burning. Keep your pans in good health by cleaning them properly and gently with soapy water. We recommend picking up a good set of saucepans and a small and a large frying pan.

MIXING BOWLS

A couple of mixing bowls will come in handy time and time again. We'd suggest getting at least two, a smaller one and a large one will see you through most kinds of recipes. Smaller bowls give you more control when you're whisking ingredients and larger bowls mean more room to mix it up.

KITCHEN KNIVES

Every kitchen needs a good set of knives. If you can, invest in some good quality, super-sharp knives – blunt knives have a habit of bouncing off ingredients, which can make them more dangerous than sharper ones. You'll need to mind your fingers with super-sharp knives too, but you'll be glad you invested when you've got knives that glide through veg, saving you so much time and effort.

KNIFE SHARPENER

Once you've invested in your sharp knives, you'll want to keep them that way! Keep them nice and sharp so you can carry on slicing and dicing like a pro.

CHOPPING BOARDS

As well as protecting your surfaces, a good set of chopping boards are the key to a safe and hygienic kitchen. We'd suggest picking up a full set of colour-coordinated chopping boards, with separate boards for veg, meat, fish and dairy. They'll make it so much easier to keep your ingredients separate, and most sets are easy to clean and tidy away once your meal prep is sorted.

POTATO MASHER

Used in a number of recipes, you'll need a decent masher to make sure you've got smooth, creamy mash to spoon onto our dishes.

FOOD PROCESSOR / BLENDER / STICK BLENDER

We like to make sauces from scratch, so a decent blender or food processor is a lifesaver. A stick blender can be used on most occasions if you're looking for something cheaper or more compact. It's well worth the investment for the flavour of all those homemade sauces.

TUPPERWARE *and* PLASTIC TUBS

Most of the Pinch of Nom recipes in this book are freezable and ideal for batch cooking. It's a good idea to invest in some freezer-proof tubs – and they don't have to be plastic. For a more eco-friendly solution, choose glass storage containers; just remember to check they're freezer-safe.

Note on plastic: We have made a conscious effort to reduce the amount of non-reusable plastic such as cling film when making our recipes. There are great alternatives to cling film now available, such as silicone stretch lids, beeswax food covers, fabric food covers and biodegradable food and freezer bags.

RAMEKIN DISHES

One of the best ways to handle portion control on sweet treats or desserts is to serve up your puddings in individual portions. By making dishes in small ramekins, you not only give yourself a set portion (which makes calorie counting so much easier), but it also makes the food look super faaaaancy!

OVENWARE

For many of the recipes you'll need either an oven tray, roasting tin or oven dish. We'd recommend making sure you've got some baking trays, square and round cake tins, a loaf tin, a large, heavy-based casserole dish with a lid, a pie dish, quiche dish and lasagne dish as essential items. Keep your ovenware in tip-top condition for longer by lining them with non-stick baking paper before cooking.

If a specific size of dish is essential to the success of a recipe, we've listed this as 'Special Equipment'.

HOB

We cook on an induction hob. If you have a gas/ceramic/hot-plate hob you may have to cook dishes for a little longer.

FINE GRATER

Using a fine grater is one of those surprising revelations. You won't believe the difference between grating cheese with a fine grater versus a standard grater. 45g of cheese, for example, can easily cover an oven dish when using a fine grater. You can also use it for citrus zest, garlic and ginger – it helps a little go a long, long way.

GARLIC CRUSHER

You'll never miss the faff of finely chopping garlic once you've invested in a garlic crusher, plus it helps spread the flavour evenly through the dish. They're relatively cheap to pick up – once you've tried one, you won't go back.

MEASURING SPOONS

Want to make sure you never get muddled between a tsp and tbsp? Pinch of Nom has absolutely, definitely never made this mistake. Honest. But these days we're never without a trusty set of measuring spoons, which help make sure it's not a tablespoon of chilli when it should have been a teaspoon. Just make sure you use a butter knife to level off the spoon – you'll be surprised how much extra you add when the spoonful is heaped.

HEATPROOF MEASURING JUG

A measuring jug is essential for measuring out wet ingredients. We recommend getting a heatproof version that you can stick in the microwave when needed.

KITCHEN KIT
(that's nice to have)

1. SLOW COOKER

We're big fans of slow cookers. You can make dishes like our Slow-Cooker All-Day Breakfast (page 54) with ease – simply throw in your ingredients, go out, enjoy your day and return to a home-cooked meal that's ready and waiting for you. They're a relatively inexpensive bit of kit that will save you a lot of time.

We use a 3.5-litre slow cooker – please don't attempt to make dishes in a slow cooker that is any smaller than this.

2. AIR FRYER

Air fryers have become a slimming staple in recent years and are the ultimate in convenience. They give you crispy, deep-fried textures and flavours without having to plunge your food into high-calorie oils. Air-fried food cooks more quickly and efficiently – which is good news for your energy bills too. If your air fryer doesn't have a preheat function, heat it at cooking temperature for a few minutes before air-frying your food.

3. ELECTRIC PRESSURE COOKER

A pressure cooker is a great investment if you're looking to save time and energy. The high-pressure cooking process creates perfectly tender meat and makes stews taste as though they've been bubbling away for hours. We recommend electric models for safety and ease of use.

Five steps for...
COOKING ON A BUDGET

Making money-saving meals shouldn't have to mean missing out on flavour or repeating the same few recipes every week. From getting savvy with your shopping, to cooking in bigger batches, there's always a way to stretch the budget and still enjoy delicious, home-cooked food. Once you've mastered cooking on a budget you'll be tucking into great-tasting recipes that workaround your life and help your pennies go that little bit further.

1. MEAL PLAN

Starting the week with a plan is a great way to get ahead and prevent any unnecessary expense. When you head to the supermarket with a meal plan and a shopping list, it makes it so much easier to stick to your food budget. Plan your meals around any fridge or freezer food that needs using up, to keep food waste to a minimum. The Pinch of Nom Planners are the perfect addition to your weekly routine, to make sure your meals are planned to perfection!

2. SHOP SMART

It's always a good idea to plan meals that are based around seasonal ingredients. Fresh fruit and veggies are so much cheaper when they're in season, and when they're not, consider using tinned or frozen versions to keep costs down. They have just as much flavour and nutrients, and they're often a fraction of the price of fresh. We also love to

scan the reduced section every time we go to the supermarket – you never know what you'll find, and you might just get lucky with something off your list!

3. TRY A VEGGIE DAY

Meat and fish are often the most expensive ingredients in any recipe. In this book we've made sure to use cheaper cuts and bulk out recipes with plenty of veggies, so you never feel like you're compromising. Including a couple of meat-free recipes in your meal plan each week can really make a difference to your spending, and you could discover a few new flavours along the way!

4. LOVE YOUR STORE CUPBOARD AND FREEZER

These are your best friends when it comes to budget cooking. From tinned food to herbs

and spices, you'll be surprised how much flavour can come from ingredients that you already have in the house. Stock up your freezer by cooking in bigger batches, so you'll end up with extra portions for another day. Another top tip is to freeze any bits of extra ingredients that might otherwise go to waste – things like slices of lemon, crushed garlic and fresh herbs can all be frozen for future use.

5. TRY NEW COOKING METHODS

Even the way you cook can affect your budget, especially with energy costs on the rise. Rather than cooking something low and slow in the oven, consider if you can use your slow cooker or pressure cooker, if you have one. Air fryers can use much less energy than heating up your whole oven, so it's well worth using these as often as possible too.

We recommend planning batch-cooking sessions where you can make multiple meals at the same time, so you only need to reheat them throughout the week.

Mains

BLT PASTA SALAD

🕐 **10 MINS**   🍲 **12 MINS**   ✗ **SERVES 3**

PER SERVING:
419 KCAL / 57G CARBS

220g dried pasta
low-calorie cooking spray
6 unsmoked bacon
   medallions, trimmed of
   fat and cut into bite-sized
   chunks
1 garlic clove, peeled and
   crushed
120g quark
70g natural fat-free yoghurt
¼–½ tsp all-purpose
   seasoning
freshly ground black pepper
200g cherry tomatoes,
   halved
big handful of lettuce ripped
   into large pieces (you can
   use any type, iceberg,
   Romaine etc.)

With just a handful of ingredients, you can serve this BLT Pasta Salad for a simple lunch, or a light evening meal. Inspired by one of our favourite sandwich fillings, it's so easy to throw together, and always a treat to eat. The creamy, yoghurt-based sauce is a great alternative to mayonnaise, and it really helps to cut down on calories. This recipe keeps well in the fridge for a couple of days, so it's handy to make a big batch on busy weeks!

Weekly Indulgence

Cook the pasta according to the packet instructions. Drain and refresh under cold running water to cool down. Drain well.

While the pasta cooks, spray a frying pan with low-calorie cooking spray and place over a medium heat. Add the bacon and garlic and fry for 3–4 minutes until nicely browned, turning the medallions halfway through. Place to one side.

Mix the quark, yoghurt and all-purpose seasoning together in a large bowl, then season with some freshly ground black pepper.

Add the bacon, tomatoes and cooked pasta to the quark mix and stir well.

Stir in the lettuce, check the seasoning and enjoy!

TIP: All-purpose seasoning is a general seasoning that can be used to enhance flavours in most dishes. It is usually found in the supermarket spice aisle.

FREEZE ME

PATTIES ONLY

GLUTEN FREE

USE GF BAPS

LOADED CURRY BURGER

🕐 **7 MINS** 🗑 **16 MINS** ✕ **SERVES 4**

PER SERVING:
376 KCAL / 38G CARBS

FOR THE ONION BHAJIS
1 small red onion, peeled and
 thinly sliced
40g sweet potato, peeled
 and grated
¼ tsp ground cumin
¼ tsp ground coriander
¼ tsp garam masala
½ medium egg, beaten
sea salt and freshly ground
 black pepper, to taste
low-calorie cooking spray

FOR THE BURGERS
400g 2%-fat minced turkey
1 tsp curry powder
½ tsp garlic granules
½ tsp onion granules
½ tsp ground coriander
½ tsp ground cumin
½ tsp ground ginger
½ tsp garam masala
½ medium egg, beaten
low-calorie cooking spray

TO SERVE
4 white baps, about 60g
 each, sliced in half
2 tbsp light mayo
1 tbsp mango chutney
3 tbsp fat-free Greek-style
 yoghurt
2g fresh coriander, finely
 chopped
50g lettuce

TO ACCOMPANY *(optional)*
Homemade Oven Chips (from
 the Pinch of Nom website,
 + 96 kcal per serving)

We just know these burgers will go down a treat with the whole family. Once you've tried them with our moreish coriander yoghurt sauce, family burger night will never be the same again! We've kept things slimming friendly without compromising on flavour by swapping out beef for lower-fat turkey burger patties. Piled high with an onion bhaji and mango chutney mayo, our favourite Indian-inspired Fakeaway flavours are in every bite.

Weekly Indulgence ————————————

To make the onion bhajis, place the onion, sweet potato, cumin, coriander, garam masala and egg in a bowl. Season with salt and pepper and mix to combine.

Spray a frying pan with low-calorie cooking spray and place over a medium heat. Split the onion bhaji mixture into four and make four rough mounds in the pan. Flatten and cook for 4 minutes. Flip over and cook for a further 4 minutes. Once cooked, remove the pan from the heat.

While the bhajis are cooking, add the burger ingredients to a mixing bowl and stir to incorporate the spices through the turkey mince. Split the mixture into four and shape into four burger patties.

Spray a frying pan with low-calorie cooking spray and add the burgers. Cook for 4 minutes on each side.

While the burgers cook, lightly toast the inside of the baps.

Mix the mayo and mango chutney together and spread the bottom of each bap with a little of the mixture. Add the yoghurt and coriander to a small bowl and stir until fully combined.

Place some lettuce on top of the mayo mixture, then a burger patty and onion bhaji. Finish with the yoghurt and serve with Homemade Oven Chips, if you like.

LASAGNE

🕐 **20 MINS**　🍲 **1 HR**　✗ **SERVES 6**

PER SERVING:
392 KCAL / 36G CARBS

SPECIAL EQUIPMENT
**30 x 20cm (12 x 8in)
ovenproof dish**

6 dried lasagne sheets

FOR THE MEAT SAUCE
low-calorie cooking spray
1 onion, peeled and diced
1 celery stick, chopped
1 medium carrot, peeled
　and chopped
2 garlic cloves, peeled
　and crushed
400g 5%-fat minced beef
1 tbsp dried mixed herbs
1 tbsp Worcestershire sauce
　or Henderson's relish
1 courgette, diced
1 red pepper, deseeded
　and diced
1 green pepper, deseeded
　and diced
4 large mushrooms, sliced
70g tomato puree
1 x 400g tin chopped
　tomatoes
200ml beef stock (1 beef
　stock cube dissolved in
　200ml boiling water)

FOR THE WHITE SAUCE
500g fat-free natural yoghurt
2 medium eggs
½ tsp mustard powder
120g reduced-fat Cheddar,
　grated
sea salt and freshly ground
　black pepper, to taste

To keep the cost and the calories down, our Lasagne recipe is packed full of fresh vegetables. This way, you can still enjoy every layer of rich, minced beef, creamy sauce, pasta and that all-important cheesy topping. One of the trickiest bits of making a slimming-friendly lasagne is getting the white sauce just right. We've tried all sorts of hacks, from blitzed cottage cheese to quark, but this is the best one so far. It's well worth giving it a go!

Everyday Light ───────────────

To make the meat sauce, spray a large frying pan (with a lid) with low-calorie cooking spray and place over a medium heat. Add the onion, celery, carrot and garlic to the pan and cook for a few minutes, until they start to soften.

Add the mince and cook until it starts to brown, breaking it up with a wooden spoon. Add the herbs and Worcestershire sauce and continue to cook for a few more minutes.

Add the courgette and peppers and give the mixture a stir. Then add the mushrooms and fry for about 5 minutes.

Stir in the tomato puree, tinned tomatoes and beef stock. Put the lid on the pan and simmer for 20–30 minutes. Adjust the seasoning if necessary.

Spread a layer of the mince mixture on the bottom of the ovenproof dish, then add a layer of lasagne sheets. Repeat until you reach the top of the dish, ending with a layer of lasagne sheets. Make sure you leave enough room for the sauce. Preheat the oven to 210–220°C (fan 190–200°C/gas mark 6–7).

To make the white sauce, mix the yoghurt, eggs, mustard powder and salt to taste. Beat well to make sure the mixture is smooth.

Pour this sauce over the top of the lasagne sheets, then sprinkle with the grated cheese. Cook in the oven for 25–30 minutes.

Remove from the oven and allow to rest for 5–10 minutes, so that it is easier to portion. Enjoy!

CHILLI BEAN SOUP

🕐 **10 MINS**　　🍲 **25 MINS**　　✕ **SERVES 6**

VEGGIE

FREEZE ME

GLUTEN FREE

USE GF STOCK CUBE

PER SERVING:
142 KCAL / 18G CARBS

SPECIAL EQUIPMENT
Stick blender

low-calorie cooking spray
1 onion, peeled and diced
1 red pepper, deseeded and diced
2 garlic cloves, peeled and crushed
1 red chilli, deseeded and diced
1 x 400g tin chopped tomatoes
500ml boiling water
1 vegetable stock cube
¼ tsp ground coriander
¼ tsp ground cumin
¼ tsp chilli powder
1 tbsp tomato puree
1 x 400g tin kidney beans, drained and rinsed
1 x 400g tin butter beans, drained and rinsed
handful of fresh coriander leaves
40g reduced-fat feta cheese
1 lime, cut into wedges

TO ACCOMPANY *(optional)*
60g crusty wholemeal bread roll (+ 144 kcal per serving)

This is a super simple soup that you can have ready to eat in 35 minutes! Using the flavours of a traditional vegetarian chilli con carne we have created a warming bowl of soup perfect for any lunchtime.

Everyday Light ————————

Spray a saucepan with low-calorie cooking spray and place over a medium heat. Add the onion and fry for 3 minutes until starting to soften. Add the pepper, garlic and chilli and fry for a further 2 minutes.

Pour in the chopped tomatoes and boiling water and crumble in the stock cube. Add the coriander, cumin, chilli powder and tomato puree and give the pan a good stir.

Bring to the boil then lower the heat, add half the kidney beans and half the butter beans and simmer for 15 minutes.

Using a stick blender blitz the soup until smoother but still chunky. Add in the remaining kidney beans and butter beans and simmer for a further 5 minutes until heated through.

Sprinkle over the fresh coriander and crumble over the feta cheese. Serve with the lime wedges, and a wholemeal bread roll, if wished.

TIP: If your soup is a little too thick add an extra splash of water.

FREEZE
ME

GLUTEN
FREE

USE GF
STOCK CUBES

CARBONARA RISOTTO

🕐 **10 MINS**   🍲 **40 MINS**   ✕ **SERVES 4**

PER SERVING:

423 KCAL / 64G CARBS

low-calorie cooking spray
200g gammon steak, visible
  fat removed and meat cut
  into small pieces
1 large onion, peeled and
  finely chopped
2 garlic cloves, peeled and
  crushed
300g Arborio risotto rice
1.4 litres stock (1 chicken and
  1 vegetable stock cube
  dissolved in 1.4 litres boiling
  water)
200g mushrooms, sliced
2 tbsp white wine vinegar
30g Parmesan cheese, finely
  grated
90g reduced-fat cream
  cheese
sea salt and freshly ground
  black pepper, to taste
handful of fresh parsley
  leaves, chopped, to serve
  (optional)

We've brought together two classic Italian-style dishes to create this incredible Carbonara Risotto. Soft Arborio rice, mushrooms and gammon, simmered in a silky, garlicky cheese sauce – this dish tastes far more indulgent than it really is. You won't need anything fancy to rustle it up either; it's super easy and perfect for a midweek meal. Like any risotto, it takes a little more time to make, but the pay-off is a super creamy, flavour-packed dinner.

Weekly Indulgence

Spray a large frying pan with low-calorie cooking spray and place over a medium heat. Add the gammon pieces, onion and garlic and cook for 5 minutes until the onion begins to soften and the gammon is seared.

Add the rice and cook for a further 3 minutes.

Begin to ladle in the stock. Add two ladlefuls and stir well. Once the liquid has absorbed add more and repeat. It will take around 30 minutes to add all the stock.

While the risotto is cooking, take a separate frying pan and spray with low-calorie cooking spray. Cook the mushrooms for 5 minutes over a medium heat until they have some colour and set aside.

When you get to the last few ladles of stock add in the mushrooms, white wine vinegar and Parmesan. Keep stirring well.

At the end add in the cream cheese and stir a few more times over the heat so it combines well. Season with salt and pepper and serve with parsley if you like.

VEGAN

FREEZE ME

DAIRY FREE

GLUTEN FREE

USE A GF STOCK CUBE

BATCH FRIENDLY

MUSHROOM *and* SPINACH CURRY

🕐 **15 MINS**   🍲 **50 MINS**   ✕ **SERVES 4**

PER SERVING:
167 KCAL / 17G CARBS

SPECIAL EQUIPMENT
Food processor

1 onion, peeled and roughly chopped
4 garlic cloves, peeled
1 red chilli, deseeded (or leave in if you like it extra spicy)
3cm (1¼in) piece of root ginger, peeled and roughly chopped
low-calorie cooking spray
1 tbsp garam masala
2 tbsp tomato puree
450g mushrooms (we used chestnut but any firm variety will do), cut into bite-sized pieces
500ml unsweetened almond milk
1 vegetable stock cube
25g ground almonds
150g sweet potato, peeled and grated
2 tsp cider vinegar
150g baby spinach
handful of fresh coriander, chopped

TO ACCOMPANY *(optional)*
50g uncooked basmati rice, cooked according to packet instructions (+ 173 kcal per serving)

Our Mushroom and Spinach Curry turns out so luxuriously creamy, you won't believe it's slimming friendly. We've used almond milk and ground almonds to give it a silky sauce texture without ramping up the calories too much. Rich with moreish nutty flavours and jam-packed with protein, you'll want this vegan-friendly wonder on your midweek menu time and time again!

Everyday Light

Place the onion, garlic, chilli and ginger into a food processor and blitz to a paste.

Spray a large saucepan or wok with low-calorie cooking spray and place over a medium-low heat. Add the paste and cook gently for 10 minutes, stirring regularly.

Add the garam masala and continue cooking for 2 minutes.

Stir in the tomato puree, then add the mushrooms and cook for another 2 minutes.

Add the almond milk and crumble in the stock cube (no need to make up the stock cube with boiling water).

Add the ground almonds and sweet potato, bring to the boil and then turn the heat down to a simmer. Cook for 30–35 minutes, stirring occasionally, until the sauce is rich and thick.

Add the cider vinegar and then stir in the spinach until it is wilted. Stir in the coriander and serve with basmati rice, if you like.

COWBOY PIE

🕐 **15 MINS**　📦 **1 HR**　✕ **SERVES 4**

PER SERVING:
453 KCAL / 61G CARBS

SPECIAL EQUIPMENT
18 x 27cm (7 x 10½in) ovenproof dish

low-calorie cooking spray
8 low-fat sausages
1 onion, peeled and chopped
1 tbsp BBQ seasoning
1 tsp garlic granules
½ tsp smoked paprika
½ tsp mustard powder
1 x 400g tin chopped tomatoes
200ml chicken stock
  (1 chicken stock cube
  dissolved in 200ml
  boiling water)
1 tbsp balsamic vinegar
1 tbsp Henderson's relish or
  Worcestershire sauce
2 carrots, peeled and
  thinly sliced
salt
700g potatoes, peeled and
  cut into small chunks
1 x 400g tin mixed beans,
  drained and rinsed
40g reduced-fat Cheddar,
  grated

TO ACCOMPANY *(optional)*
80g steamed green
  vegetables (+ 35 kcal per
  serving)

This unmissable Cowboy Pie is made up of sausages and beans in a rich, tangy barbecue sauce, topped with fluffy mash and golden cheese. We've used low-fat sausages and reduced-fat Cheddar cheese to keep this recipe nice and low in calories, without losing out on flavour. It's a comforting, hearty meal that's fantastic for batch cooking. You'll want to make a few extra portions and stock up the freezer for a rainy day!

Weekly Indulgence

Spray a frying pan with low-calorie cooking spray, place over a medium heat, add the the sausages and brown for 5 minutes. They don't need to be cooked through, just browned. Pop them on a plate and set aside.

Give the pan a wipe and spray with a little more cooking spray. Sauté the onion for 5 minutes until soft.

Add the BBQ seasoning, garlic granules, smoked paprika and mustard powder. Stir well, then add the tomatoes, stock, balsamic vinegar and Henderson's relish.

Cut each sausage into four and add to the pan along with the carrots. Bring to the boil, reduce the heat and simmer for 20 minutes, until the carrots and sausages are cooked.

Meanwhile, add some salt to a pan of boiling water and cook the potatoes for around 15 minutes. The potatoes are cooked when a knife slides easily into them. Drain and mash.

Preheat the oven to 200°C (fan 180°C/gas mark 6).

When the carrots and sausages are cooked, stir in the beans and pour the mix into the ovenproof dish. Top with the mashed potato and sprinkle with the grated cheese. Bake for 20–25 minutes until the top is golden.

Serve with steamed vegetables or your choice of accompaniment.

CHICKEN FAJITA PASTA

🕐 **10 MINS**   🍲 **20 MINS**   ✕ **SERVES 4**

USE DF YOGHURT

USE GF PASTA

PER SERVING:
491 KCAL / 78G CARBS

400g dried pasta
1 tbsp ground cumin
1 tbsp ground coriander
1–2 tsp chilli powder, to taste
½ tsp dried chilli flakes
1 tsp garlic salt
low-calorie cooking spray
2 small skinless chicken
  breasts, sliced into strips
2 tbsp tomato puree
2 peppers (any colour),
  deseeded and sliced
1 onion, peeled and sliced
200ml water
fat-free yoghurt, to serve
  (optional)

We LOVE Mexican-inspired flavours, and this easy, speedy recipe is a great way to turn your favourite dish into a family-sized, freezer-friendly dinner. Forget tortilla wraps – mixing fajita-spiced chicken and veggies into some freshly cooked pasta gives it a whole new lease of life. On the table in just half an hour, this dish is perfect for batch cooking; any leftovers will make for a delicious lunch the next day!

Weekly Indulgence

Cook the pasta according to the packet instructions. In a bowl, mix the cumin, coriander, chilli powder, chilli flakes and garlic salt until thoroughly combined.

Spray a frying pan with low-calorie cooking spray and place over a medium heat. Add the sliced chicken and cook for 5 minutes. Add the spice mix and tomato puree and cook for 3 minutes.

Add the sliced peppers and onion along with the water and mix well. Leave to cook for 10 minutes until the chicken is cooked through and the peppers and onion have just started to soften.

Drain the pasta and combine with the chicken fajita mix. Serve with a dollop of fat-free yoghurt, or a different topping of your choice!

FREEZE ME

GLUTEN FREE

USE GF PASTA

CREAMY PASTA WITH BACON, PEAS *and* MUSHROOMS

🕐 **10 MINS**   🍲 **20 MINS**   ✕ **SERVES 2**

PER SERVING:
532 KCAL / 81G CARBS

200g dried pasta
2 smoked or unsmoked
  bacon medallions, trimmed
  of fat and cut into strips
150g white mushrooms, sliced
2 garlic cloves, peeled and
  crushed
150g frozen peas
sea salt and freshly ground
  black pepper, to taste
100g reduced-fat cream
  cheese
5g Parmesan cheese, finely
  grated

Nothing tastes quite as indulgent as a creamy pasta dish for dinner. With bacon, mushrooms and sweet garden peas, you'll be surprised just how slimming friendly this recipe is. You only need a handful of ingredients to put this dish together – grab your trusty bag of frozen peas and any kind of dried pasta that's left over in the cupboard and get ready to turn them into something really special. It's delicious, good for you and good for your pocket too!

Special Occasion ────────────────

Cook the pasta according to the packet instructions.

Add the bacon strips and mushrooms to a non-stick saucepan and cook over a medium heat for 4–5 minutes until tender. Add the garlic and cook for a further couple of minutes, keeping a close eye on it to ensure the garlic does not burn.

Add the frozen peas and stir well. Season generously with salt and pepper – remembering that the bacon can be salty. Turn down the heat to low and stir in the cream cheese and Parmesan. Do not let it boil or the cheese will burn.

Once the pasta is cooked, drain, add to the sauce and stir until thoroughly coated – enjoy!

FREEZE ME

DAIRY FREE

BATCH FRIENDLY

CHILLI MEATBALL ORZO

🕐 **20 MINS** 🍲 **VARIABLE** (SEE BELOW) 🍴 **SERVES 6**

PER SERVING:
356 KCAL / 40G CARBS

SPECIAL EQUIPMENT
Food processor, mini chopper or coarse grater

FOR THE MEATBALLS
1 medium slice wholemeal bread
500g 5%-fat minced beef
1 small onion, peeled and finely chopped
1 garlic clove, peeled and crushed
1 tsp mild chilli powder
1 small egg, beaten with a fork
sea salt and freshly ground black pepper, to taste
low-calorie cooking spray

FOR THE SAUCE
1 onion, peeled and chopped
1 medium green pepper, deseeded and chopped
1 medium red pepper, deseeded and chopped
2 garlic cloves, peeled and crushed
2 tsp mild chilli powder
1 tsp smoked paprika
1 tsp ground cumin
1 x 400g tin chopped tomatoes
1 tbsp tomato puree
600ml beef stock (1 beef stock cube dissolved in 600ml boiling water)
1 x 400g tin kidney beans, drained and rinsed
200g orzo
10g flat-leafed parsley, roughly chopped

Can't decide what to have for dinner? This is the best of all worlds! It's a combo of chilli con carne and meatballs with pasta, but, because it uses orzo, it reminds us of a risotto too. To keep the recipe slimming friendly, we've used reduced-fat mince and plenty of veggies. This means that you get a super hearty, filling and delicious dinner, all for 358 calories! It freezes well too, making this dish a batch-cooking dream.

Everyday Light

HOB-TOP METHOD
🍲 **45 MINS**

To make the meatballs, place the bread in a food processor or mini chopper and blitz to fine breadcrumbs. Alternatively, you can use a coarse grater to do this.

Place the minced beef, onion, garlic, chilli powder, breadcrumbs, egg and some salt and pepper in a medium mixing bowl. Use clean hands to mix together well. Divide into twelve equal pieces and shape into twelve meatballs.

Spray a large, deep frying pan with low-calorie cooking spray. Place over a medium heat. Add the meatballs and cook for 4–5 minutes, turning, to seal and lightly brown on all sides. Remove the sealed meatballs from the frying pan and place on a plate. Set aside.

To make the sauce, add the onion and peppers to the frying pan, stir and fry over a medium heat for 10–15 minutes, until the onion and peppers soften. Add the garlic, chilli powder, paprika and cumin, stir and cook for a further 1–2 minutes. Lower the heat and add the tinned tomatoes, tomato puree, beef stock, kidney beans and orzo to the pan. Season well with salt and pepper. Stir well, then place the sealed meatballs in the sauce.

Cover with a lid or cover tightly with foil. Simmer gently over the lowest heat for 20–25 minutes, stirring occasionally, until piping hot throughout.

The meatballs should be cooked through and have no pinkness inside, the orzo should be tender, and the sauce should be thickened slightly. Stir in the parsley and serve.

SLOW-COOKER METHOD
⬛ 4 HRS 20 MINS – 4 HRS 40 MINS

SPECIAL EQUIPMENT
Slow cooker

To make the meatballs, place the bread in a food processor or mini chopper and blitz to fine breadcrumbs. Alternatively, you can use a coarse grater to do this.

Place the minced beef, onion, garlic, chilli powder, breadcrumbs, egg, and some salt and pepper in a medium mixing bowl. Use clean hands to mix together well. Divide into twelve equal pieces and shape into twelve meatballs.

Spray a large, deep frying pan with low-calorie cooking spray. Place over a medium heat. Add the meatballs and cook for 4–5 minutes, turning, to seal and lightly brown on all sides. Remove the sealed meatballs from the frying pan and place on a plate. Set aside.

To make the sauce, add the onion and peppers to the frying pan. Stir and fry over a medium heat for 10–15 minutes, until the onion is golden and the peppers soften.

Add the garlic, chilli powder, paprika and cumin, stir and cook for a further 1–2 minutes. Transfer the vegetable mixture from the frying pan into the slow cooker.

Add the tinned tomatoes, tomato puree and beef stock to the slow cooker. Season well with salt and black pepper. Stir well, then place the sealed meatballs in the sauce. Don't stir the meatballs.

Cover with the lid and cook on low for 3½–4 hours. Don't stir the mixture during this cooking time otherwise you may break up the meatballs.

After 3½–4 hours add the kidney beans and orzo and gently stir in, making sure the kidney beans and orzo are submerged in the sauce.

Replace the lid and increase the setting to high. Continue to cook for a further 20–25 minutes, stirring once, until the meatballs are cooked through and have no pinkness inside, the orzo is tender, the beans are piping hot, and the sauce is thickened slightly. Stir in the parsley and serve hot.

COTTAGE PIE

 20 MINS   **55 MINS**   ✕ **SERVES 4**

PER SERVING:
361 KCAL / 40G CARBS

SPECIAL EQUIPMENT
Large shallow ovenproof dish,
approx. 30 x 20cm (12 x 8in)

low-calorie cooking spray
500g 5%-fat minced beef
1 large onion, peeled and
   chopped
3 large carrots, peeled and
   chopped
500ml beef stock (2 beef
   stock cubes dissolved in
   500ml boiling water)
1 tbsp Worcestershire sauce
   or Henderson's relish
sea salt and freshly ground
   black pepper, to taste
600g potatoes, peeled and
   cut into chunks

Cottage Pie is a classic for a reason! With fluffy mash, a meaty filling and a deliciously rich gravy, it's a wholesome, hearty dinner that'll put a smile on anyone's face. Our slimming-friendly version uses lean mince and leaves out the flour that you'd find in traditional recipes – you really can't taste the difference. One of the best bits about this dish is that it's great for making in advance and heating up when you're ready. Convenient AND delicious!

Everyday Light ─────────────────

Spray a large saucepan with low-calorie cooking spray and place over a medium heat. Add the mince and fry for 5 minutes, stirring occasionally with a wooden spoon to break up any lumps, until browned. Add the onion and carrots and cook for a few more minutes.

Add the stock to the pan, then add the Worcestershire sauce and stir. Season with black pepper.

Bring to the boil, cover and simmer for 20 minutes, removing the lid for the final 5 minutes, and allow to reduce until it thickens.

While the mince mixture is cooking, cook the potatoes in a pan of salted boiling water. When they are soft remove from the heat, drain, and mash with a little salt and pepper.

Preheat the oven to 220–240°C (fan 200–220°C/gas mark 7–8). Pour the mince mixture into the ovenproof dish and allow to cool slightly. If you don't, the mash may sink through the mince.

Spoon the mashed potato onto the mince and run a fork over the top to cover the meat and give some texture. Alternatively you could pipe the potato onto the top.

Place in the preheated oven and cook for 25–30 minutes or until golden brown.

Serve with an accompaniment of your choice.

PESTO *and* GREEN BEAN SPAGHETTI

🕐 **5 MINS**　🗑 **15 MINS**　✗ **SERVES 4**

VEGGIE

USE VEGGIE
HARD CHEESE

VEGAN

USE VEGAN
HARD CHEESE

**GLUTEN
FREE**

USE GF
SPAGHETTI

PER SERVING:
210 KCAL / 34G CARBS

SPECIAL EQUIPMENT
Food processor

150g dried spaghetti
170g new potatoes, sliced
100g green beans, trimmed
60g fresh basil
4 garlic cloves, peeled
30g Parmesan cheese, finely
　grated
juice of 1 lemon

Our take on a north Italian pasta alla Genovese, this Pesto and Green Bean Spaghetti is a thrifty game-changer. Using just a few simple ingredients and one saucepan, you won't believe how easy it is to prepare this spaghetti dish from scratch. By combining Parmesan with garlic, basil and zesty lemon juice, we've recreated a luscious green pesto sauce for a fraction of the calories (and price!) of shop-bought versions. Don't forget to save your pasta water – it gives every twisty forkful an even silkier texture.

Everyday Light ————————————

Add the spaghetti and new potatoes to a large saucepan of boiling water. Cook for 8 minutes until the potatoes and spaghetti are nearly done. Add the green beans and cook for another 4 minutes.

While the spaghetti is cooking, add the basil, garlic, Parmesan cheese and lemon juice to a food processor. Blitz until smooth.

Once the spaghetti, potatoes and green beans are cooked, drain (reserving a little of the cooking water).

Add the spaghetti, potato and green beans back to the pan and pour over the pesto mixture. Add 1 tablespoon of the reserved pasta water, stir and add a few extra tablespoons of water as needed (see Tip). The pesto should coat each spaghetti strand. Serve.

TIP: We added 3 tablespoons of the reserved pasta water to coat our pasta, but it depends on how thick your pesto is. Start with 1 tablespoon and go from there.

USE GF WRAPS

FAJITA BOMBS

 10 MINS **25 MINS** ✕ **SERVES 6**

PER SERVING:
379 KCAL /31G CARBS

low-calorie cooking spray
650g skinless chicken breasts,
  chopped into small chunks
1 pepper, any colour,
  deseeded and finely diced
½ red onion, peeled and
  finely diced
2 tsp ground coriander
2 tsp ground cumin
1 tsp smoked paprika
1 tsp chilli powder
1 tsp garlic granules
2 tbsp tomato puree
200g tinned chopped
  tomatoes
6 low-calorie soft tortilla
  wraps
100g reduced-fat Cheddar,
  finely grated

TO SERVE
200g tinned chopped
  tomatoes
½ red onion, peeled and
  finely diced
1 tsp lime juice
½ tsp garlic granules
6 tbsp reduced-fat sour
  cream

If fajitas are a family favourite in your house, you need to try this fun twist on the midweek classic! Bake in the oven until the shell is all crispy, and then crack them open for an explosion of fajita flavours! Our recipe uses a homemade fajita spice blend, which is SO much tastier and more budget friendly than the pre-packaged mixes you get in the supermarket. We've even included salsa and sour cream to add right before serving!

Everyday Light ──────────────────

Preheat the oven to 200°C (fan 180°C/gas mark 6).

Spray a frying pan with low-calorie cooking spray and place over a medium heat. Add the chicken to the pan and fry for 3 minutes, then add the pepper and onion and cook for 3 more minutes.

Sprinkle in the coriander, cumin, paprika, chilli powder and garlic granules and give the pan a stir to coat the chicken in the spices. Add in the tomato puree and chopped tomatoes and allow to bubble for 4 minutes.

Microwave the tortilla wraps for 30 seconds. This is to make them easier to fold (see Tip for using the hob).

Lay a tortilla wrap out and sprinkle with 1 tablespoon of Cheddar cheese. Spoon over one sixth of the chicken mixture on top of the cheese. Fold the bottom of the tortilla over the chicken, folding it away from yourself, then rotate and repeat the fold on the next edge. Continue until the chicken is contained within the tortilla.

Place the fajita bomb in an oven dish with the seam facing down. Repeat with the other tortillas.

Sprinkle the remaining cheese on the top and pop in the oven for 15 minutes until the cheese is melted and the tortilla wraps are just starting to go crispy.

In a small bowl make a salsa by combining the chopped tomatoes, red onion, lime juice and garlic granules. Serve the tortilla bombs with a spoonful of the salsa and sour cream.

TIP: You can also heat the tortilla wraps in a frying pan over a medium heat – simply heat each wrap for 20–30 seconds, flipping over halfway through.

SLOW-COOKER ALL-DAY BREAKFAST

🕐 10 MINS   🍲 2 HRS   ✕ SERVES 4

PER SERVING:
352 KCAL /23G CARBS

SPECIAL EQUIPMENT
Slow cooker

low-calorie cooking spray
8 bacon medallions (smoked or unsmoked), trimmed of all fat
4 reduced-fat pork sausages
1 x 420g tin reduced sugar and salt baked beans
200g button mushrooms
200g cherry tomatoes
4 medium eggs
sea salt and freshly ground black pepper, to taste

You might have tried our popular Air-fryer Full English, but how about a version that you can leave to cook for a couple of hours, while you run errands? Come back to a hearty breakfast of bacon, sausages, eggs, beans, mushrooms and tomatoes, all cooked in your slow cooker. It took a lot of practice to get this method perfect, so you'll need to follow it closely! If you don't fancy hard-boiled eggs, just leave them out and scramble, fry or poach them separately right before serving.

Everyday Light ────────────────────

Spray the inside of the slow cooker with low-calorie cooking spray.

Stick the bacon medallions around the inner wall of the slow-cooker pot and line up the sausages along the edge, standing up. You need to leave as much room as possible on the base of the pot.

Peel the outer paper label off the tin of beans and remove the lid. Stand the tin in the slow cooker against the sausages to keep them in place.

Take a sheet of foil and place the mushrooms onto it. Spray with low-calorie cooking spray and season with salt and pepper. Scrunch it into a pouch and place into the slow cooker.

Take another sheet of foil and place the tomatoes onto it. Spray with low-calorie cooking spray and season with salt and pepper. Scrunch it into a pouch and place into the slow cooker.

Scrunch a piece of foil and place into the bottom of the remaining space in the cooker. Place your eggs in their shells on top of it so they are standing up.

Place the lid on the slow cooker and set to high for 2 hours.

When ready, remove the eggs and run them under cold water. Peel them and cut in half before adding to the plate. Add the rest of the ingredients to the plates and serve.

TIPS: We use a 3.5-litre slow cooker for our recipes. If yours is smaller you may not be able to fit everything in. You need to use a standard thickness sausage rather than chipolatas in this recipe or they may overcook, resulting in a crumbly texture.

SPICY SAUSAGE *and* TOMATO RICE

 10 MINS 🍲 30 MINS ✕ SERVES 4

PER SERVING:
402 KCAL / 70G CARBS

300g basmati rice
low-calorie cooking spray
1 red onion, peeled and finely diced
3 garlic cloves, peeled and crushed
1 medium red pepper, deseeded and finely diced
4 reduced-fat chicken chipolata sausages, sliced
2 tsp hot chilli powder
2 tsp smoked paprika
1 tsp dried oregano
1 tsp dried parsley
2 tsp tomato puree
2 tsp sriracha sauce
700ml boiling water
1 x 400g tin chopped tomatoes
sea salt and freshly ground black pepper, to taste
40g reduced-fat feta cheese
1 lime, cut into wedges

We can't get over how easy it is to rustle up this one-pot wonder! Your sausages, veggies and rice all go into the same pan, where they simmer away until everything's cooked to perfection. We've relied on a few trusty store-cupboard herbs and spices to load this dish with flavour and a medium fiery heat. If you like your food a bit milder, simply miss out the sriracha or go easy on the chilli powder.

Weekly Indulgence ————————————

Place the rice in a sieve and rinse under cold running water until the water runs clear. Set to one side to drain.

Spray a large, deep frying pan with low-calorie cooking spray and place over a medium heat. Add the onion and garlic and fry for 3 minutes until just softening. Add the red pepper and sausages and continue to fry for a further 4 minutes, until the sausages are browned.

Once the vegetables are soft add the chilli powder, paprika, oregano, parsley, tomato puree and sriracha sauce. Fry for a minute until the spices become fragrant.

Add the boiling water, chopped tomatoes and rice, and give the pan a stir.

Bring to the boil, then lower the heat to a simmer. Cover with a lid or tight-fitting foil. Cook for 6 minutes, stir, re-cover, and cook for a further 6 minutes. Stir the pan again, re-cover, and cook for a final 6 minutes. Turn off the heat and leave the pan to stand for 5 minutes.

Remove the lid or foil and season to taste with salt and pepper. Crumble over the feta cheese and serve with the lime wedges.

FISH FINGER PIE

🕐 **15 MINS**   🍲 **40 MINS**   ✕ **SERVES 4**

PER SERVING:
490 KCAL / 64G CARBS

SPECIAL EQUIPMENT
18 x 27cm (7 x 10½in) ovenproof dish

low-calorie cooking spray
4 large potatoes, about 200g each, peeled and cut into large chunks
60ml semi-skimmed milk
100g reduced-fat mature Cheddar, finely grated
10 frozen breadcrumbed cod or haddock fish fingers
sea salt and freshly ground black pepper, to taste
1 x 415g tin reduced sugar and salt baked beans in tomato sauce

FOR THE TOPPING
20g reduced-fat mature Cheddar, finely grated

TO ACCOMPANY *(optional)*
80g steamed green vegetables (+ 35 kcal per serving)

Put those fish fingers from the back of the freezer to good use and rustle up this Fish Finger Pie for a midweek meal that the whole family will love. You'll only need a few simple ingredients, and we bet you already have most of them in the kitchen! Layers of fish fingers, beans, cheese and mashed potatoes mean that this recipe is total comfort food. It tastes amazing and it's minimal effort – the dream combination!

Special Occasion ————————————————

Preheat the oven to 210°C (fan 190°C/gas mark 6). Line a baking tray with foil and grease with a little low-calorie cooking spray. Grease the ovenproof dish with a little low-calorie cooking spray.

Put the potatoes in a large saucepan of cold water and cover with a lid. Place over a high heat and bring to the boil, taking care not to let the water boil over. Reduce the heat to medium, partially cover with the lid and simmer for 20 minutes until tender when tested with a knife.

Drain the potatoes well and return to the saucepan off the heat. Mash well with the milk and 50g of the Cheddar cheese. Season well with salt and pepper. Set aside.

While the potatoes are cooking, cook the fish fingers. Arrange them on the prepared baking tray and place in the preheated oven for 10 minutes or according to the packet instructions, until cooked through.

To assemble the pie, place the cooked fish fingers in the bottom of the greased ovenproof dish and spread out evenly.

Pour the baked beans over the fish fingers. Sprinkle over the remaining 50g Cheddar cheese in an even layer.

Add the mashed potato, spreading it over the cheese. Texture the top with a spoon or fork and sprinkle over the 20g Cheddar. Place the ovenproof dish on a baking tray.

Bake in the oven for about 20 minutes until golden brown on top and piping hot throughout. Serve with steamed vegetables or an accompaniment of your choice.

VEGGIE QUESADILLAS

🕐 **20 MINS**　　🍲 **VARIABLE** (SEE BELOW)　　✕ **SERVES 6**

VEGGIE

VEGAN

USE DF
CHEESE

PER SERVING:
302 KCAL / 34G CARBS

FOR THE SALSA
2 small tomatoes, finely diced
1 roasted red pepper (from a
  jar in vinegar), drained and
  finely diced
10g fresh coriander, finely
  chopped
1 tsp sriracha or chilli sauce

FOR THE GUACAMOLE
1 avocado, flesh only, mashed
  with a fork
1 garlic clove, peeled and
  crushed
10g fresh coriander, finely
  chopped
½ tsp lime juice
sea salt and freshly ground
  black pepper, to taste

FOR THE QUESADILLAS
1 x 400g tin black beans,
  drained and rinsed
1 x 200g tin sweetcorn,
  drained
6 low-calorie soft tortilla
  wraps
120g reduced-fat Cheddar,
  finely grated
low-calorie cooking spray

TO ACCOMPANY (optional)
Homemade Oven Chips (from
  the Pinch of Nom website,
  + 96 kcal per serving)

These Veggie Quesadillas are so packed with flavour, you'll never miss the meat. Folded into neat triangles (using a handy hack we saw on TikTok!) you get fresh salsa, creamy guacamole, melted cheese and crunchy vegetables in every bite. You can make these really quickly in a frying pan or crisp them up in your air fryer – either way, they're completely delicious and perfect for a speedy lunch or dinner.

Everyday Light ——————————————————

HOB-TOP METHOD
🍲 **4 MINS**

Mix the salsa ingredients together and set aside.

Mix the guacamole ingredients together and set aside.

Mix together the beans and sweetcorn and set aside.

Take a tortilla wrap and cut a line from the bottom edge to the centre. Imagine the hour hand at 6 o'clock, that's where the cut should be!

Now imagine your wrap is in quarters. Add a sixth of the guacamole to one quarter, then a sixth of the beans and sweetcorn to another, a sixth of the cheese to another and a sixth of the salsa onto the last.

Fold the quarter next to the cut upward so it is over the quarter above it. Then fold that over the third quarter, and finish by folding over the last quarter so you have a triangle. Now repeat for the rest of the wraps until they are all done!

Spray your frying pan with low-calorie cooking spray and place over a medium heat. When the pan is hot, add your quesadillas and spray the tops with more low-calorie cooking spray. You will probably need to do this in batches!

After 2 minutes cooking, flip the quesadillas over to cook for 2 minutes on the other side. When cooked, they will have a nice golden colour and the cheese inside should be melted.

Serve with Homemade Oven Chips, or a side of your choice.

AIR-FRYER METHOD
🍳 5–7 MINS

SPECIAL EQUIPMENT
Air fryer

Preheat your air fryer to 180°C (see Tip below).

Mix the salsa ingredients together and set aside.

Mix the guacamole ingredients together and set aside.

Mix together the beans and sweetcorn and set aside.

Take a tortilla wrap and cut a line from the bottom edge to the centre. Imagine the hour hand at 6 o'clock, that's where the cut should be!

Now imagine your wrap is in quarters. Add a sixth of the guacamole to one quarter, then a sixth of the beans and sweetcorn to another, a sixth of the cheese to another and a sixth of the salsa onto the last.

Fold the quarter next to the cut upward so it is over the quarter above it. Then fold that over the third quarter, and finish by folding over the last quarter so you have a triangle. Now repeat for the rest of the wraps until they are all done!

Spray your quesadillas with some low-calorie cooking spray and place into the air fryer. Cook for 5–7 minutes, until the outside is crispy and the cheese has melted. You will probably need to do this in batches!

Serve with Homemade Oven Chips, or a side of your choice.

TIP: If your air fryer doesn't have a preheat function, we suggest heating at cooking temperature for a few minutes before air-frying your food.

HUNTER'S CHICKEN PASTA BAKE

🕐 **15 MINS**   🍲 **20 MINS**   ✕ **SERVES 6**

PER SERVING:
293 KCAL / 33G CARBS

200g dried pasta, we used fusilli but any pasta shape will work
low-calorie cooking spray
1 red onion, peeled and diced
1 medium red pepper, deseeded and diced
2 garlic cloves, peeled and crushed
350g diced chicken breast
4 smoked or unsmoked bacon medallions, cut into strips
1 x 400g tin chopped tomatoes
2 tsp BBQ seasoning
1 tsp garlic granules
1 tsp onion granules
¼ tsp chilli powder
¼ tsp mustard powder
1 tbsp balsamic vinegar
1 tbsp Henderson's relish or Worcestershire sauce
1 tbsp tomato puree
2 tsp white granulated sweetener
1 chicken stock cube
40g reduced-fat Cheddar, finely grated

Imagine all the cheesy, saucy barbecue flavour of the pub-grub classic, combined with the comfort of a warming pasta dish. That's what you get from this hearty Hunter's Chicken Pasta Bake. We've bulked out the recipe with lots of tasty veggies and swapped to reduced-fat cheese, to keep it much lighter than the pub alternative. The seriously cheesy topping is the real winner here – when it's golden brown and bubbling, your bake is ready to dish up!

Everyday Light ————————————————

Preheat the oven to 220°C (fan 200°C/gas mark 7).

Cook the pasta according to the packet instructions. Drain when cooked and leave to one side.

While the pasta is cooking, spray a large frying pan with low-calorie cooking spray and place over a medium heat. Add the onion and fry for 4 minutes until softened, add the pepper and garlic and continue to fry for 2 minutes.

Add the diced chicken and bacon and brown on all sides. Add the chopped tomatoes, BBQ seasoning, garlic granules, onion granules, chilli powder, mustard powder, balsamic vinegar, Henderson's relish, tomato puree and sweetener. Give the pan a good stir and crumble in the stock cube.

Allow the pan to bubble for 5 minutes until the sauce has thickened.

Add the drained pasta and stir to coat in the sauce. Tip into a medium ovenproof dish and sprinkle on the cheese. Pop into the oven for 8 minutes until the cheese is bubbly and golden.

VEGGIE

 VEGAN

USE VEGAN
YOGHURT

 FREEZE ME

 GLUTEN FREE

 BATCH FRIENDLY

MUSHROOM MASALA

 10 MINS   **22 MINS**   ✕ **SERVES 4**

PER SERVING:
132 KCAL /18G CARBS

low-calorie cooking spray
1 large onion, peeled and
   thinly sliced
1cm (½in) piece of root
   ginger, peeled and finely
   grated
4 garlic cloves, peeled and
   crushed
2 tsp garam masala
½ tsp ground cumin
1 tsp ground coriander
½ tsp ground turmeric
250ml boiling water
600g white mushrooms,
   quartered
1 x 400g tin chopped
   tomatoes
2 tbsp tomato puree
3 tbsp fat-free yoghurt,
   Greek-style or natural
sea salt and freshly ground
   black pepper, to taste
pinch of granulated
   sweetener, to taste

TO ACCOMPANY (optional)
50g uncooked basmati rice,
   cooked according to packet
   instructions (+ 173 kcal per
   serving)

This warming Mushroom Masala is bursting with so much Indian-inspired flavour, you won't miss the meat. A dream to rustle up for a midweek family Fakeaway night, it goes from pan to plate in under half an hour. Our homemade masala sauce combines fresh veggies with basic store-cupboard herbs and spices, keeping it fuss-free to make and budget friendly too. So satisfying and versatile, this comfort food curry is perfect for batch cooking.

Everyday Light

Place a frying pan over a medium heat and spray well with low-calorie cooking spray. Add the onion, ginger, garlic, garam masala, cumin, coriander and turmeric and cook for 2 minutes to release the aromatics.

Add 50ml of the boiling water to deglaze the bottom of the pan and cook the onion for another 5 minutes to soften it.

Add the mushrooms to the pan with the tinned tomatoes and the remaining 200ml boiling water. Mix well and simmer for 15 minutes.

Stir through the tomato puree and yoghurt. Season with salt and pepper and sweetener to taste.

Serve with rice or your choice of accompaniment.

FREEZE
ME

GLUTEN
FREE

USE GF
PASTA AND
STOCK CUBE

LEMON CHICKEN *and* SPINACH PASTA

🕐 **10 MINS**   🍲 **30 MINS**   ✗ **SERVES 4**

PER SERVING:
269 KCAL /27G CARBS

low-calorie cooking spray
280g skinless chicken breasts,
  cut into strips
1 garlic clove, peeled and
  chopped
250ml chicken stock
  (1 chicken stock cube
  dissolved in 250ml boiling
  water)
juice of 2 lemons
½ tsp dried thyme
150g dried tagliatelle
30g light spreadable cheese
160g spinach, washed and
  chopped
½ tsp freshly ground black
  pepper
salt
30g Parmesan cheese, grated
lemon wedges, to serve
  (optional)

With an indulgent-tasting, creamy sauce, this quick and easy Lemon Chicken and Spinach Pasta is a delicious dinner that you can pull together in only 40 minutes! Chopped-up fresh spinach adds extra nutrition, and we've brought it all together with a squeeze of zesty lemon juice. We think tagliatelle works well for mopping up creamy sauces, but you could swap this out for your preferred pasta shape. Try penne or farfalle, or whatever you have in the cupboard!

Everyday Light —————————————

Spray a frying pan with low-calorie cooking spray, add the chicken and fry for 5–10 minutes on a medium heat, until golden brown.

Add the garlic and cook for another minute. Add the chicken stock to the pan along with the lemon juice and thyme and cook for 3–5 minutes.

While the chicken is cooking, cook the pasta according to the packet instructions and drain.

Add the light spreadable cheese to the stock and mix well. Then add the spinach, black pepper and drained pasta and mix into the sauce. Cook for a further minute.

Season to taste with salt and pepper, sprinkle with Parmesan and serve with extra lemon wedges if you like.

BOMBAY-STYLE POTATO *and* CHICKEN TRAYBAKE

🕐 **20 MINS***   🗑 **40 MINS**   ✕ **SERVES 2**

*PLUS 30 MINS MARINATING

PER SERVING:

546 KCAL / 46G CARBS

SPECIAL EQUIPMENT

32cm (13in) roasting tray

FOR THE MARINADE

90g fat-free Greek-style
  yoghurt
2 tsp tomato puree
2 tsp mango chutney
1 tsp garam masala
½ tsp garlic granules
½ tsp ground cumin
½ tsp ground coriander
1 tsp lemon juice

FOR THE TRAYBAKE

4 bone-in chicken thighs,
  skin and visible fat removed
300g new potatoes
sea salt and freshly ground
  black pepper, to taste
1 small red onion, peeled
  and sliced
1 red pepper, deseeded
  and sliced
200g tinned chickpeas,
  drained and rinsed
low-calorie cooking spray
bunch of fresh coriander,
  roughly chopped
lemon wedges, to garnish
  (optional)

You can't go wrong with a traybake when you fancy a fuss-free dinner, and this one always delivers on flavour. We've nestled some succulent chicken thighs onto an oven tray, along with fragrant, spiced potatoes, chunky veggies and chickpeas. Our homemade, Indian-inspired yoghurt marinade is what brings this whole recipe to life, adding aromatic spices and a hint of fresh lemon.

Special Occasion ————————————————

Mix together the marinade ingredients. Rub half the marinade into the chicken thighs, place them on a plate, cover and allow to marinate in the fridge for 30 minutes (you can leave them longer if you like).

Cut any large potatoes in half, or quarters if they are very large. You want them evenly sized, in no more than 4cm (1½in) chunks. Place in a pan of cold salted water, bring to the boil and cook for 6 minutes. Drain well and leave for a couple of minutes to steam dry.

Preheat the oven to 200°C (fan 180°C/gas mark 6).

Place the parboiled potatoes, onion, pepper and chickpeas in the roasting tray. Add the remaining yoghurt marinade and toss around until well coated. Nestle the marinated chicken thighs into the potatoes and season with a little salt and pepper, if required.

Spritz with some low-calorie cooking spray and place in the middle of the oven. Cook for 35–40 minutes, until the potatoes are golden brown and soft in the middle, and the chicken thighs are cooked through, with no pink remaining.

Sprinkle over the coriander before serving, with some lemon wedges for garnish (optional).

TIPS: If you like it fiery, add some chilli powder to the marinade. Alternatively, you can add a chopped chilli to the tray before roasting. If you are scaling this up to serve more than two, you will probably need to cook it a little longer.

VEGGIE

VEGAN

USE VEGAN
STOCK POT

FREEZE
ME

DAIRY
FREE

MARMITE PASTA

🕐 **5 MINS**   🍲 **15 MINS**   ✕ **SERVES 2**

PER SERVING:
394 KCAL / 68G CARBS

low-calorie cooking spray
1 leek, trimmed and thinly
   chopped into rings
1–2 red onions, peeled and
   cut into half moons
150g dried spaghetti (or any
   shape pasta)
1 vegetable stock pot
1–2 tbsp Marmite (entirely
   dependent on how
   Marmitey you want it)

If you love Marmite, you'll love this easy-peasy dinner!
Ready in just 20 minutes, you'll only need a handful of
ingredients to end up with a plateful of delicious, savoury
pasta. We've made ours using spaghetti, but this recipe
will work with absolutely any shape of pasta, so just grab
whatever's in the cupboard! If you're a big fan, feel free
to be a little more generous with the Marmite – you're in
charge of how strong you'd like the flavour.

Everyday Light ────────────────────

Put water on to boil for the pasta.

Spray a frying pan with low-calorie cooking spray and
place over a medium heat. Add the leek and onions and fry
for 10–15 minutes until soft and golden.

While the leek and onions are frying, cook the pasta
according to the packet instructions.

Once the pasta is cooked, drain the water, leaving a little
bit in the pan – not too much otherwise it will be too
watery. Add the vegetable stock pot, Marmite and fried
vegetables and mix until combined.

That's it! Really simple, quick and adaptable. Enjoy!

TIP: This recipe is quite high
in salt, so you could choose
to opt for reduced-salt yeast
extract instead of Marmite.

USE HENDERSON'S RELISH

MEATBALL MASH BAKE

🕐 **20 MINS**　🍲 **45 MINS**　✕ **SERVES 4**

PER SERVING:

414 KCAL / 43G CARBS

SPECIAL EQUIPMENT

18 x 28cm (7 x 11in) ovenproof dish

FOR THE MASH

600g potatoes, peeled and quartered
sea salt and freshly ground black pepper, to taste
2 tbsp tomato puree
1 tbsp balsamic vinegar
40g reduced-fat Cheddar, finely grated

FOR THE MEATBALLS

500g 5%-fat minced beef
1 tbsp Henderson's relish or Worcestershire sauce
1 tsp onion granules

FOR THE SAUCE

low-calorie cooking spray
2 onions, peeled and thinly sliced
3 garlic cloves, peeled and crushed
300g mushrooms, sliced
1 x 400g tin chopped tomatoes
1 tsp dried basil
1 tsp dried oregano
pinch of granulated sweetener

Our Meatball Mash Bake is everything it says on the tin. A handy midweek alternative to lasagne or cottage pie, it gives two comfort food staples a run for their money. Baked in the oven until the Cheddar cheese topping is bubbly and golden, we've layered our mashed potato over a bed of homemade Italian-style meatballs. To make the hearty filling extra special, we've prepared a rich, tomato-based sauce that tastes far too good to be so simple.

Weekly Indulgence

Preheat the oven to 210°C (fan 190°C/gas mark 6).

Place the potatoes in a saucepan and cover with cold water. Season the cooking water with salt. On the stove bring the pan to the boil. Reduce the heat so it is gently boiling for 15 minutes, or until the potatoes are cooked through and tender. Remove from the heat and drain the water.

Add the tomato puree and balsamic vinegar to the potatoes, then mash until smooth. Season with salt and pepper to taste and set aside.

While the potatoes are cooking, take a bowl and mix the meatball ingredients. Use clean hands to incorporate the mix and then shape into small meatballs, around 3cm (1¼in) wide.

Spray a large frying pan with low-calorie cooking spray and place over a medium heat. Add the onions and garlic and cook for 5 minutes until beginning to soften.

Add the meatballs to the pan and cook for 10 minutes until browned all over.

Add the mushrooms, chopped tomatoes, basil and oregano and mix well. Cook for another 5 minutes until the mushrooms begin to soften. Season with salt and pepper to taste, and add a pinch of sweetener.

Pour the meatball mixture into the bottom of the ovenproof dish and spread out evenly. Spoon the mash onto the top of the meatballs and spread it using a fork. Sprinkle over the cheese and place into the oven for 15 minutes, until the cheese is melted and the top is browned. Serve.

MINCED BEEF HOTPOT

 15 MINS   **1 HR 20 MINS**   ✕ **SERVES 4**

PER SERVING:
417 KCAL / 51G CARBS

SPECIAL EQUIPMENT
30 x 20cm (12 x 8in) ovenproof dish

800g potatoes, peeled and sliced

low-calorie cooking spray

1 onion, peeled and finely diced

500g 5%-fat minced beef

4 medium carrots, peeled and finely diced

1 tbsp Henderson's relish or Worcestershire sauce

1 tsp red wine vinegar

½ tsp dried thyme

350ml beef stock (2 beef stock cubes dissolved in 350ml boiling water)

100g frozen peas

1 tbsp cornflour mixed to a slurry with 1 tbsp water

sea salt and freshly ground black pepper, to taste

We love an easy dinner that doesn't leave behind loads of washing up. This Minced Beef Hotpot is cheap, tasty, simple to make and only uses one pan and an oven dish. Hidden under the golden, baked potato topping is a satisfying mixture of onions, vegetables and 5%-fat minced beef in a deep, rich gravy. Hearty and comforting, you can leave this to bubble away in the oven until you're ready to tuck in.

Weekly Indulgence ————————————————

Place the sliced potatoes in a large microwavable bowl, cover with water and microwave on full power for 5 minutes. Drain them carefully and set aside. (See Tip below if you want to cook them on the hob instead.)

Preheat the oven to 200°C (fan 180°C/gas mark 6).

Spray a large frying pan with some low-calorie cooking spray and place over a medium heat. Add the diced onion and fry for about 5 minutes until it starts to soften. Add in the mince and continue cooking for another 5 minutes, stirring with a wooden spoon to break up any lumps. Add the carrots and cook until the mince has started to brown.

Stir in the Henderson's relish, red wine vinegar and thyme, then add the beef stock. Bring to the boil and allow to simmer for 10 minutes. The liquid should reduce by about half.

Stir in the peas. Add the cornflour slurry and bring to a bubble until thickened.

Check the seasoning, then pour the thickened mince mixture into the ovenproof dish and top with the sliced potato, arranging the potato slices in overlapping rows.

Season the potato with some salt and black pepper, then cover with foil and cook in the oven for about 35 minutes. Remove the foil and return to the oven for another 25 minutes or so, until the potatoes are cooked through and golden brown. Remove from the oven and serve.

TIP: If you don't have a microwave, you can cook the potatoes on a hob. Add the sliced potatoes to a saucepan and cover with cold water. Bring the water to the boil then lower the heat and simmer for 5–8 minutes until the potato slices are soft when a knife is inserted but still holding their shape. Drain.

CHICKEN TIKKA NACHOS

🕐 **10 MINS**   🍲 **15 MINS**   ✕ **SERVES 4**

PER SERVING:
359 KCAL /42G CARBS

170g lightly salted tortilla
  chips

FOR THE CHICKEN TIKKA
1 tsp smoked paprika
½ tsp ground coriander
½ tsp ground cumin
¼ tsp garam masala
¼ tsp ground turmeric
¼ tsp garlic granules
¼ tsp onion granules
sea salt and freshly ground
  black pepper, to taste
1 medium skinless chicken
  breast, about 130g, cut into
  2cm (¾in) dice
low-calorie cooking spray
1 small red onion, peeled and
  diced
1 medium red pepper,
  deseeded and diced

FOR THE TOP
40g reduced-fat Cheddar
  cheese, finely grated
4 tbsp fat-free Greek-style
  yoghurt
1 tbsp lemon juice
2g fresh mint, finely chopped
2g fresh coriander, finely
  chopped
2 tbsp mango chutney

Ready for a family-friendly Fakeaway recipe with a twist? We've mashed together two of our favourite takeaway orders to create this lightly spiced sharing dish. A layer of crunchy tortilla chips is topped with tikka-spiced chicken, golden cheese and a drizzle of mint and coriander yoghurt. Just wait until you smell this bubbling under the grill – you won't believe it's slimming friendly (and so much cheaper than ordering from the takeaway!).

Everyday Light

In a small bowl, combine the paprika, coriander, cumin, garam masala, turmeric, garlic granules, onion granules and a pinch each of salt and pepper. Add the chicken and stir to coat in the spices.

Spray a frying pan with low-calorie cooking spray and set the pan on a medium heat. Add the onion and red pepper and fry for 4 minutes. Add the coated chicken breast pieces and continue to fry for 5 minutes until the chicken is cooked through and shows no sign of pinkness.

Preheat the grill. Spread the tortilla chips over a baking tray. Add the cooked onion, pepper and chicken mixture. Sprinkle over the grated cheese.

Pop the tray under the grill for 4–6 minutes until the cheese is golden brown.

Add the yoghurt, lemon juice, mint and coriander to a small bowl and mix to combine. Once the cheese is melted and golden, drizzle the yoghurt mixture over the nachos.

Spoon over the mango chutney and serve!

VEGGIE

 FREEZE ME

 GLUTEN FREE

USE GF PASTA

SNEAKY MAC *and* CHEESE

 10 MINS   **20 MINS**   ✕ **SERVES 6**

PER SERVING:
235 KCAL / 30G CARBS

SPECIAL EQUIPMENT
Blender or stick blender

400g cauliflower, broken into
   florets
150g light spreadable cheese
½ tsp onion granules
½ tsp garlic granules
½ tsp mustard powder
200g dried macaroni or other
   dried pasta
2 courgettes, peeled and cut
   into 1cm (½in) cubes
low-calorie cooking spray
sea salt and freshly ground
   black pepper, to taste
80g reduced-fat Cheddar
   cheese, finely grated
   (optional)

FOR THE TOP *(optional)*
1 spring onion, chopped
drizzle of sriracha sauce

This Sneaky Mac and Cheese gets its name from all of the hidden veggies that we've packed into it. Peeled and cubed courgette replaces some of the pasta, and cooked cauliflower helps to make the sauce thick and creamy, so that you still get a big cheesy portion without all of the extra calories. Ideal for any fussy eaters, this recipe is a fantastic way to get more veggie goodness into your diet without even noticing!

Everyday Light ——————————————

Add the cauliflower to a saucepan of boiling water and cook for 10 minutes until soft.

Once the cauliflower is cooked, drain the water and add to a blender with the spreadable cheese, onion granules, garlic granules and mustard powder (you could also place in a separate bowl and use a stick blender). Blend until smooth and set aside.

While the cauliflower is cooking, add the pasta to another pan of boiling water and cook according to the packet instructions. Drain, reserving a few tablespoons of the cooking water.

Add the courgettes to the pan that the cauliflower was cooked in and spritz with low-calorie cooking spray. Gently sauté over a medium heat for 5 minutes until softened and cooked through. They should be as soft as the cooked pasta.

Pour the sauce into the pan with the courgettes, along with the drained pasta and the reserved pasta water. Stir to combine and season with salt and pepper.

You can serve the dish like this, or make it extra cheesy by spooning it into a medium ovenproof dish (or several small ones) and topping with the grated Cheddar. Place under a preheated grill for 5 minutes until the top is bubbling and golden and serve with an optional sprinkle of spring onion and a drizzle of sriracha sauce.

FREEZE ME

CHICKEN *and* SPRING VEGETABLE ORZOTTO

🕐 **10 MINS**   🗑 **25 MINS**   ✕ **SERVES 4**

PER SERVING:
400 KCAL / 46G CARBS

low-calorie cooking spray
1 small leek, trimmed and
  thinly sliced
400g diced chicken breast
1 tsp garlic granules
1 tsp dried Italian herbs
700ml chicken stock
  (2 chicken stock cubes
  dissolved in 700ml boiling
  water)
250g orzo
150g green beans, halved
75g frozen broad beans or
  peas
juice of ½ lemon
30g Parmesan cheese, grated
freshly ground black pepper

TO ACCOMPANY (optional)
75g mixed green salad
  (+ 15 kcal per serving)

An irresistible addition to your midweek menu, our Chicken and Spring Vegetable Orzotto has all the creamy indulgence of a risotto for far less effort. Stir occasionally for half an hour and let the springtime flavours really soak in. With fresh veggies and a clever blend of herbs and stock, you won't believe how luxuriously silky it is without a pot of cream in sight. Finish with Parmesan and a drizzle of lemon to bring the Mediterranean-style flavours together!

Everyday Light ─────────────────

Spray a large saucepan with low-calorie cooking spray and place over a medium-high heat. Add the leek and fry for 2–3 minutes, until softened. Add the chicken and continue cooking for 5 minutes, until the chicken is sealed.

Stir in the garlic granules and herbs. Add the stock, orzo and vegetables to the pan and bring to the boil.

Reduce the heat and simmer for 12–15 minutes, stirring occasionally, until all the liquid has been absorbed.

Squeeze in the lemon juice and add the Parmesan. Stir well and season with black pepper.

Serve with a mixed green salad, if you like.

SALT *and* PEPPER CHICKEN

 10 MINS **40 MINS** **SERVES 4**

PER SERVING:
294 KCAL / 7.3G CARBS

FOR THE SALT AND PEPPER CHICKEN
8 chicken thighs or
   drumsticks – all skin and
   visible fat removed
low-calorie cooking spray
3 spring onions, finely
   chopped, plus extra to
   garnish
½ onion, peeled and finely
   chopped
½ chilli, deseeded and finely
   chopped
½ red pepper, deseeded and
   chopped

FOR THE SPICE MIX
1 tbsp sea salt flakes
1 tbsp granulated sweetener
   or other sweetener
1 tbsp MSG (monosodium
   glutamate), optional
   (see Tip)
½ tbsp Chinese 5-spice
good pinch of chilli flakes,
   depending on how hot
   you like it
1 tsp ground white pepper

TO ACCOMPANY *(optional)*
Homemade Oven Chips (from
   the Pinch of Nom website,
   + 96 kcal per serving)

> **TIP:** Monosodium
> glutamate or MSG is a
> flavour-enhancer commonly
> added to most Chinese food
> from the takeaway. There
> have been many debates
> about the use of MSG, so if
> you prefer not to use it you
> can just leave it out.

Tender chicken seasoned with a spicy coating, it's no wonder this Chinese-inspired dish is simply irresistible. Our version is easy to make and ready within an hour, so you'll have it on the table faster than ordering from the takeaway (and you'll know exactly what's gone into it too!). You can alter the amount of chilli to make this as fiery or mild as you like. The spice mix is really versatile and you get plenty of it in this recipe, so you can store the extra for next time . . . bonus!

Everyday Light

Preheat the oven to 210°C (fan 190°C/gas mark 6).

Make the spice mix by toasting the salt flakes in a hot pan until they start to brown – it's very important to do this to get the true salt and pepper flavour. Mix the toasted salt and all the other spice mix ingredients together.

Sprinkle the chicken thighs with a couple of teaspoons of the spice mix.

Place the chicken on a baking tray and cook in the oven according to the packet instructions (usually around 30 minutes), or until the juices run clear and no pink remains.

When the chicken is cooked, heat up a wok sprayed with some low-calorie cooking spray over a medium heat. Add the spring onions, onion, chilli and peppers to the wok over and cook for 3–4 minutes until they start to brown slightly.

Add the cooked chicken thighs to the wok along with 1–2 tablespoons of spice mix. Don't add it all at once, add it a bit at a time, taste and stop when it's spicy enough.

Cook through for another 3–4 minutes, then serve, sprinkled with some finely chopped spring onions, and accompanied with Homemade Oven Chips if you like.

SAUSAGE-STUFFED PASTA SHELLS

🕐 **20 MINS**   🗑 **1 HR**   ✕ **SERVES 4**

FREEZE ME

DAIRY FREE

USE DF CHEESE

BATCH FRIENDLY

PER SERVING:
345 KCAL / 47G CARBS

SPECIAL EQUIPMENT
Stick blender
18 x 27cm (7 x 10½in)
    ovenproof dish

FOR THE TOMATO SAUCE
low-calorie cooking spray
1 onion, peeled and diced
3 garlic cloves, peeled and
    crushed
1 medium red pepper,
    deseeded and diced
1 medium carrot, peeled and
    diced
150ml beef stock (1 beef
    stock cube dissolved in
    150ml boiling water)
1 tbsp Henderson's relish or
    Worcestershire sauce
1 tbsp tomato puree
1 x 400g tin chopped tomatoes
1 tsp dried mixed herbs
1 tsp white granulated
    sweetener

FOR THE PASTA
24 large, dried pasta shells,
    about 175g
4 reduced-fat pork sausages
1 tsp dried sage
1 tsp onion granules
¼ tsp sea salt
¼ tsp freshly ground black
    pepper
60g reduced-fat Cheddar,
    finely grated, for the top

TO ACCOMPANY *(optional)*
75g mixed green salad
    (+ 15 kcal per serving)

This filling dinner has got it all! The supersize pasta shells are stuffed with a moreish mixture of sausagemeat and sage, nestled in our homemade tomato sauce and topped with glorious melted cheese. We've thrown loads of veggies into our sauce, ramping up the flavour and adding extra goodness. You'll want to spoon up every last bit!

Everyday Light ─────────────────

Spray a large frying pan with low-calorie cooking spray and place over a medium heat. Add the onion and fry for 4 minutes. Add the garlic, red pepper and carrot. Fry for a further 4 minutes until softening.

Mix the beef stock with the Henderson's relish and tomato puree. Pour into the frying pan along with the chopped tomatoes, mixed herbs and sweetener, and give everything a stir to combine. Lower the heat and simmer for 15 minutes.

Meanwhile, cook the pasta in a pan of boiling salted water for a minute less than the packet instructions, then drain in a colander. Rinse under cold water to stop it from cooking further and drain well. The pasta shouldn't be completely cooked through and should still retain some bite. Set aside.

Squeeze the sausagemeat into a mixing bowl, discarding the casings. Add the sage, onion granules, salt and pepper and mix until smooth. Using a small spoon, fill the parcooked pasta shells with the sausage mixture and place on a plate.

Preheat the oven to 200°C (fan 180°C/gas mark 6).

Once the vegetables are softened and the sauce reduced, blitz with a stick blender. We left some chunky bits in our tomato sauce, but you can blitz until totally smooth if you prefer. Season to taste with salt and pepper and pour into the ovenproof dish.

Place the filled shells on top of the tomato sauce, making sure they are nestled in well. Sprinkle over the grated cheese and bake in the oven for 35 minutes, until the sausage-filled pasta is cooked and the cheese golden brown. Serve with a mixed salad, if you like.

FREEZE ME

GLUTEN FREE

USE GF MACARONI, FLOUR AND STOCK CUBE

MAC *and* CHEESE LASAGNE

🕐 **10 MINS**   🍲 **45 MINS**   ✕ **SERVES 4**

PER SERVING:
438 KCAL / 57G CARBS

SPECIAL EQUIPMENT
30 x 20cm (12 x 8in) baking dish

FOR THE MEAT FILLING
low-calorie cooking spray
1 red onion, peeled and diced
1 medium red pepper, deseeded and diced
2 garlic cloves, peeled and crushed
1 medium carrot, peeled and diced
250g 5%-fat minced beef
1 beef stock cube
150ml boiling water
1 tbsp Henderson's relish
1 tbsp tomato puree
2 tsp dried mixed herbs
1 x 400g tin chopped tomatoes

FOR THE MACARONI
200g dried macaroni
2 tbsp plain flour
200ml skimmed milk
¼ tsp mustard powder
40g reduced-fat spreadable cheese
40g reduced-fat Cheddar, finely grated
sea salt and freshly ground black pepper, to taste

TO ACCOMPANY *(optional)*
80g steamed vegetables (+ 38 kcal per serving)

Why pick one comfort food when your heart wants both? This recipe is what happens when you combine macaroni cheese with beef lasagne, and you're going to be so glad you tried it! It may not sound all that slimming friendly, but with a few clever swaps, you can dig into the ultimate comfort food dish for just 438 calories. Just wait until you try the rich, creamy, cheesy sauce . . . it's such a crowd-pleaser!

Weekly Indulgence ─────────────────

Spray a frying pan with low-calorie cooking spray and place over a medium heat. Add the onion and fry for 2 minutes. Add the pepper and garlic and fry for a further 2 minutes. Add the carrot and beef and fry for 4 minutes, stirring with a wooden spoon to break up any lumps, until the meat is browned on all sides.

Add the stock cube to the water along with the Henderson's relish, tomato puree and mixed herbs. Pour into the pan along with the chopped tomatoes. Bring to the boil then lower the heat to a simmer. Simmer for 8–10 minutes until the sauce has thickened and the vegetables are soft.

Preheat the oven to 200°C (fan 180°C/gas mark 6). Cook the macaroni according to the packet instructions and drain.

While the macaroni is cooking, add the flour to a microwavable jug along with 2 tablespoons of the milk. Whisk into a smooth paste. Add in the rest of the milk and whisk again.

Heat in 1-minute blasts in the microwave, whisking in between, until the mixture has thickened. Ours took 4 minutes, but this will depend on your microwave. Add the mustard powder, spreadable cheese and 20g Cheddar cheese and whisk until melted and smooth. Season with salt and pepper to taste.

Pour the cheese sauce over the cooked macaroni and stir to coat.

Spread the beef mixture into the bottom of the baking dish and top with the macaroni cheese. Sprinkle over the remaining Cheddar and pop into the oven for 20–25 minutes until the top is golden and bubbly. Serve with steamed green vegetables, if wished.

TIP: If you don't have a microwave you can cook the cheese sauce on the hob. Add the flour and 2 tbsp of the milk to a small saucepan and whisk into a smooth paste. Add in the rest of the milk and whisk again. Place the pan over a low heat and continue to whisk for 6–8 minutes until thickened. Be careful not to boil the mixture. Once thickened, add the mustard powder, spreadable cheese and 20g Cheddar cheese and whisk until melted and smooth. Season with salt and pepper to taste.

VEGGIE

VEGAN

USE DF
CHEESE

FREEZE
ME

DAIRY
FREE

USE DF
CHEESE

GLUTEN
FREE

USE GF
STOCK POT

BATCH
FRIENDLY

CHEESY PARSNIP SOUP

🕐 **10 MINS**   🍲 **45 MINS**   ✕ **SERVES 6**

PER SERVING:
148 KCAL /13G CARBS

SPECIAL EQUIPMENT
Stick blender

low-calorie cooking spray
1 onion, peeled and finely
    chopped
1 garlic clove, peeled and
    crushed
1 large leek, trimmed and
    roughly chopped
4 medium parsnips, about
    500g, trimmed, peeled and
    cut into 1cm (½in) pieces
1 litre vegetable stock
    (1 vegetable stock pot
    dissolved in 1 litre boiling
    water)
120g reduced-fat mature
    Cheddar, grated
sea salt and freshly ground
    black pepper, to taste

TO ACCOMPANY *(optional)*
60g wholemeal bread roll
    (+ 144 kcal per serving)

There's nothing better than a hot bowl of soup on a chilly day, especially when the soup is as cheesy as this one. Packed with veggie goodness, and super satisfying, it's a hearty lunch that'll keep you feeling full until dinnertime. Thick and creamy, we've used a reduced-fat Cheddar to cut down on calories without compromising on flavour.

Everyday Light ——————————————————

Spray a medium saucepan with low-calorie cooking spray and place over a medium heat. Add the onion and cook for 5 minutes, stirring, until translucent. Add the garlic, leek and parsnips and cook for a further 10 minutes, stirring, until the parsnips are starting to soften a little.

Add the stock and stir. Bring to the boil, lower the heat, cover and simmer for 30 minutes until the parsnips are soft.

Remove the saucepan from the heat and blitz the soup until smooth, using a stick blender.

Stir in the cheese until melted and season to taste with salt and black pepper.

Serve with a wholemeal bread roll or other accompaniment of your choice.

TIP: It's worth using a mature Cheddar to give the soup a good cheesy flavour. You can garnish each serving of soup with 5g grated reduced-fat Cheddar for an additional 16 kcal per serving (optional).

DAIRY FREE

GLUTEN FREE

USE GF SAUSAGES

SAUSAGE TRAYBAKE

🕐 **15 MINS**   🍲 **45 MINS**   ✕ **SERVES 4**

PER SERVING:
365 KCAL / 54G CARBS

500g new potatoes, halved (or cut into wedges if large)
4 medium carrots, peeled and cut into chunks about the same size as the potatoes
8 reduced-fat pork sausages
2 red onions, peeled and cut into wedges
1 eating apple, cored and sliced
low-calorie cooking spray
sea salt and freshly ground black pepper, to taste
2 tbsp honey
2 tbsp wholegrain mustard
1 tsp garlic granules
200ml apple juice
a few sprigs of fresh thyme

On busy days, it's so nice to be able to throw a few simple ingredients into a dish and let the oven work its magic. This dish is minimal in effort, but so rewarding when it comes to flavour. Drawing on the classic combination of pork and apple, our recipe uses fresh wedges of apple, nestled in with onions, carrots and potatoes. Coated in a honey and mustard sauce, all the flavours mingle together as they roast until everything's golden, caramelized and completely irresistible.

Everyday Light

Preheat the oven to 220°C (fan 200°C/gas mark 7).

Place the potatoes and carrots in a saucepan, cover with cold water and bring to the boil. Cook for 5 minutes, then drain well.

Place the sausages, onions and apple in a large roasting tin. Add the drained potatoes and carrots.

Spray well with low-calorie cooking spray, season with a little salt and black pepper and toss around to coat the vegetables evenly.

Place in the oven and cook for 20 minutes, shaking halfway through to ensure even cooking.

In a small bowl, mix together the honey, mustard, garlic granules and apple juice. Pour over the sausages and vegetables and toss around to coat well.

Add some thyme sprigs, return to the oven and cook for a further 20 minutes, until the sausages are cooked and the vegetables are browned. Serve!

CHICKEN *and* CHIPS PIE

🕐 **25 MINS** 🗑 **1 HR 10 MINS** 🍴 **SERVES 4**

FREEZE ME

CHICKEN FILLING ONLY

GLUTEN FREE

USE GF STOCK CUBE

BATCH FRIENDLY

PER SERVING:
320 KCAL / 30G CARBS

SPECIAL EQUIPMENT
18 x 27cm (7 x 10½in) ovenproof dish

FOR THE FILLING
low-calorie cooking spray
1 onion, peeled and finely chopped
1 large leek, trimmed and thinly sliced
200g white mushrooms, sliced
500g skinless, boneless chicken thighs, diced
2 tsp mustard powder
250ml chicken stock (1 chicken stock cube dissolved in 250ml boiling water)
75g reduced-fat cream cheese
½ tsp fresh thyme leaves, stalks removed and leaves finely chopped
sea salt and freshly ground black pepper, to taste

FOR THE TOP
2–3 large potatoes, approx. 500g in total, peeled
½ tsp garlic granules

TO ACCOMPANY *(optional)*
80g steamed green vegetables (+ 35 kcal per serving)

We've said goodbye to the pastry (and a fair few calories too) for this tasty take on a classic pub-grub meal. Instead of serving them on the side, we've used thick-cut, garlicky chips as the topping for our creamy chicken and mushroom pie filling. Believe us, this warming dinner tastes so good, you'd never know it was slimming friendly. You don't need any fancy ingredients either – just simple, homely bits that you'd usually pick up in your weekly shop.

Everyday Light ——————————————————

Spray a large frying pan with low-calorie cooking spray and place over a medium heat. Add the onion and leek and cook for 6–8 minutes until soft. Add the mushrooms and cook for a further 5 minutes.

Add the chicken and cook for 5 minutes until sealed, then stir in the mustard powder. Lower the heat, pour in the chicken stock and simmer, uncovered, for 10 minutes, until reduced slightly.

Remove from the heat and stir in the cream cheese and thyme until completely blended in. If the sauce seems too thin, continue to simmer, uncovered, for a few more minutes. If the sauce seems too thick, stir in a little water.

Taste the chicken mixture and season with salt and black pepper if needed. Transfer the chicken mixture into the ovenproof dish and set aside.

Meanwhile, preheat the oven to 220°C (fan 200°C/ gas mark 7). Cut the potatoes into 1cm (½in)-wide chips and place in a bowl of cold water to rinse off the starch. Drain the chips in a colander, then dry them using some kitchen towel. Place them on a baking tray and spray with low-calorie cooking spray, turning to coat all over.

Sprinkle over the garlic granules and season well with salt and black pepper, turning to coat all over.

Place the chips in the preheated oven and cook for 20 minutes, turning over once. The chips will be slightly tender at this point, but not completely cooked. Remove from the oven and set aside.

Reduce the oven temperature to 180°C (fan 160°C/gas mark 4). Arrange the chips evenly over the top of the chicken mixture and cook in the oven for 15–20 minutes, until the chips are golden and soft inside, and the pie is piping hot throughout.

Serve with steamed green vegetables or an accompaniment of choice.

TIPS: Make sure to cut the potatoes into even 1cm (½in)-thick chips, so that they cook evenly in the time stated. You can use diced chicken breast instead of chicken thighs, if you prefer.

FREEZE ME

DAIRY FREE

GLUTEN FREE

USE HENDERSON'S RELISH

GINGERED PORK

🕐 **15 MINS**　🍲 **VARIABLE** (SEE BELOW)　✗ **SERVES 4**

PER SERVING:
285 KCAL / 21G CARBS

2 tsp ground ginger
½ tsp freshly ground black pepper
½ tsp sea salt
1 tbsp cornflour
480g lean diced pork
low-calorie cooking spray
1 x 400g tin chopped tomatoes
2 medium carrots, peeled and cut into matchsticks
1 red pepper, deseeded and thinly sliced
5cm (2in) piece of root ginger, peeled and finely grated
1 tbsp tomato puree
2 tbsp Worcestershire sauce or Henderson's relish
¼ tsp sriracha sauce
1 tbsp balsamic vinegar
2 tsp granulated sweetener

TO ACCOMPANY *(optional)*
50g uncooked basmati rice, cooked according to packet instructions (+ 173 kcal per serving)

Baked in the oven or left to bubble away in the slow cooker, this one-pot Gingered Pork is a flavoursome family warmer. We've combined chopped tomatoes, vegetables, herbs and spices with punchy ginger to make our showstopping sauce, and left our pork pieces to cook until they're fall-off-the-fork tender. It tastes so mouthwateringly good, you'll be relieved to hear that it's freezer-friendly too.

Weekly Indulgence

OVEN METHOD
🍲 **1 HR 35 MINS**

SPECIAL EQUIPMENT
26–30cm (10½–12in) lidded ovenproof dish

Preheat the oven to 190°C (fan 170°C/gas mark 5).

Mix the ground ginger, pepper, salt and cornflour in a small bowl. Sprinkle over the pork and stir until the meat is coated.

Spray a frying pan with low-calorie cooking spray and place over a medium heat. Add the pork and fry until lightly browned and sealed on all sides.

Add the pork to the ovenproof dish and pour over the chopped tomatoes and 50ml of water.

Add the carrots, pepper, fresh ginger, tomato puree, Worcestershire sauce or Henderson's relish, sriracha, balsamic vinegar and sweetener and stir until combined.

Cover with a lid and cook in the oven for 1 hour 30 minutes.

Serve with basmati rice or your choice of accompaniment.

TIP: We use granulated sweetener with the same weight and texture as sugar. You can replace the amount of sweetener in this recipe for sugar and adjust the calories accordingly.

SLOW-COOKER METHOD
🍲 3 HRS

SPECIAL EQUIPMENT
Slow cooker

Mix the ground ginger, pepper, salt and cornflour in a small bowl. Sprinkle over the pork and stir until the meat is coated.

Spray a frying pan with low-calorie cooking spray and place over a medium heat. Add the pork and fry until lightly browned and sealed on all sides.

Add the pork to the slow-cooker pot and pour over the chopped tomatoes.

Add the carrots, pepper, fresh ginger, tomato puree, Worcestershire sauce or Henderson's relish, sriracha, balsamic vinegar and sweetener and stir until combined.

Set the slow cooker to high and cook for 3 hours.

Serve with basmati rice or your choice of accompaniment.

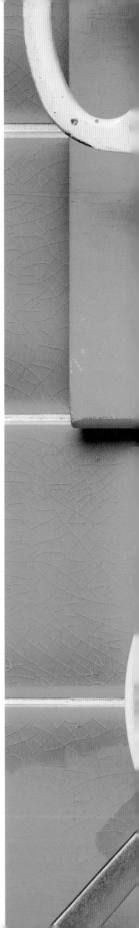

TUNA *and* TOMATO SPAGHETTI

🕐 **10 MINS**   🍲 **25 MINS**   ✕ **SERVES 4**

PER SERVING:
380 KCAL / 57G CARBS

low-calorie cooking spray
300g cherry tomatoes, halved
sea salt and freshly ground black pepper, to taste
1 red onion, peeled and finely chopped
2 garlic cloves, peeled and crushed
1 tsp dried Italian herbs
300g dried spaghetti
2 x 145g tins tuna chunks in brine, drained
40g baby spinach leaves

FOR THE TOP
20g Parmesan cheese, finely grated

Who knew you could turn a couple of tins of tuna into this hearty, Italian-inspired delight? Using ingredients that you'll usually have in your store cupboard, we've created this bowlful of delicious tomatoey pasta. Thrifty and fuss-free, you'll rustle up this recipe time and time again. Roasting your cherry tomatoes in the oven creates a more intense flavour, with a sweetness that brings the whole dish together. Don't forget a good sprinkle of Parmesan cheese right before serving!

Everyday Light ———————————————

Preheat the oven to 240°C (fan 220°C/gas mark 8). Line a large baking tray with a sheet of foil and spray with low-calorie cooking spray.

Place the halved cherry tomatoes in a single layer, cut side up, on the lined baking tray. Spray with low-calorie cooking spray and season with salt and black pepper.

Place the tomatoes in the oven for 10–15 minutes, until slightly wrinkled and starting to caramelize at the edges.

Remove from the oven and set aside.

While the tomatoes are roasting, spray a frying pan with low-calorie cooking spray and place over a medium heat. Add the onion and fry for about 10 minutes, until softened.

Add the garlic and dried Italian herbs, stir and cook for a further 1–2 minutes.

Cook the spaghetti in a large saucepan of boiling water, for about 10 minutes or according to the packet instructions. Drain well and return to the saucepan.

Add the onion mixture, roasted tomatoes, tuna chunks and spinach to the spaghetti in the saucepan. Season well with salt and black pepper and stir until the spinach has just wilted.

Divide the Tuna and Tomato Spaghetti among four warmed pasta dishes. Sprinkle with grated Parmesan cheese and serve at once.

TIP: Cook the spaghetti until it's just tender or 'al dente'. This will take about 10 minutes, or follow the cooking instructions on the packet.

CHILLI MAC 'n' CHEESE

🕐 **15 MINS** 🗑 **45 MINS** ✕ **SERVES 6**

PER SERVING:
528 KCAL / 57G CARBS

low-calorie cooking spray
2 onions, peeled and finely
  diced
2 carrots, peeled and diced
500g 5%-fat minced beef
4 garlic cloves, peeled and
  crushed
2 tsp mild chilli powder
1 tsp ground cumin
1 tsp dried oregano
2 x 400g tins chopped
  tomatoes
2 peppers, any colour,
  deseeded and diced
2 tbsp tomato puree
2 tbsp Henderson's relish
600ml beef stock (2 beef
  stock cubes dissolved in
  600ml boiling water)
300g dried macaroni
1 x 400g tin kidney beans,
  drained and rinsed
180g reduced-fat mature
  Cheddar, grated
small handful of fresh
  coriander, chopped
  (optional)

Borrowing the best bits from two of our favourite comfort foods, this epic Chilli Mac 'n' Cheese is a batch-cook sensation. Using reduced-fat Cheddar cheese, extra-lean mince and plenty of nutritious veggies, this hearty one-pot wonder tastes deliciously indulgent. We've kept things on the milder side with a couple of teaspoons of chilli powder, but there's nothing to stop you turning up the heat if you're feeling brave. Don't forget to save freezer-friendly portions for a rainy day!

Special Occasion

Spray a large saucepan with low-calorie cooking spray and place over a medium heat. Add the onions and carrots and sauté for 5 minutes until softened.

Add the mince and cook for a further 5 minutes, stirring with a wooden spoon to break up any lumps, until the mince is no longer pink.

Add the garlic, chilli powder, cumin and oregano and stir in for 1 minute until the spices become fragrant. Add the chopped tomatoes, peppers, tomato puree, Henderson's relish and stock, and bring to the boil. Turn down the heat to medium-low, cover with a tight-fitting lid and simmer for 20 minutes, until the carrots are soft.

Add the macaroni to the pan, stir well and replace the lid. Allow to cook for a further 10–12 minutes, until the pasta is just cooked.

Stir in the beans and cheese, reserving a little cheese to garnish if you wish, allowing 2 minutes for the beans to heat through and the cheese to melt.

Stir in the coriander, if using, and serve!

FREEZE ME

DAIRY FREE

USE DF HARD CHEESE

GLUTEN FREE

USE GF SPAGHETTI, STOCK CUBES AND HENDERSON'S RELISH

BATCH FRIENDLY

SPAGHETTI BOLOGNESE

 10 MINS **40 MINS** ✗ **SERVES 8**

PER SERVING:
428 KCAL / 63G CARBS

low-calorie cooking spray
500g 5%-fat minced beef
1 carrot, peeled and grated
150g mushrooms, sliced
1 courgette, grated
1 large onion, peeled and finely diced
1 leek, trimmed and finely diced
1 x 400g tin chopped tomatoes
4 garlic cloves, peeled and crushed
1 tbsp dried oregano
1 tbsp dried basil
2 tbsp tomato puree
400g passata
1 tbsp Worcestershire sauce or Henderson's relish
2 beef stock cubes, crumbled
600g dried spaghetti
sprinkle of grated Parmesan cheese, to serve

When it comes to pasta, you can't go wrong with a good Spag Bol! Everyone has their own version, and we think our slimming-friendly recipe is one of the best out there. We've tweaked and perfected it over the years, most recently adding in some extra veg to bulk it out. Not only does this make the meat go further (gotta love a thrifty meal), it's also an excellent way of sneaking some extra goodness into your dinner.

Weekly Indulgence

Spray a large saucepan with low-calorie cooking spray and place over a medium heat. Add the mince, stirring with a wooden spoon to break up any lumps, and cook for 5 minutes. Add all of the veg, chopped tomatoes, garlic and herbs and cook over a low heat for a further 5 minutes.

Stir in the tomato puree and cook for a couple of minutes. Add the remaining ingredients, apart from the spaghetti, and stir well. Simmer over a low heat for 30 minutes, stirring occasionally, until the sauce is thick and rich, and the meat is tender.

Meanwhile, bring a large pan of salted water to the boil and cook the pasta according to the packet instructions.

Serve the sauce immediately with the spaghetti and a sprinkle of Parmesan!

HONEY SOY CHICKEN THIGHS

🕐 **5 MINS*** 🍲 **1 HR** ✕ **SERVES 4**

*PLUS 1 HR MARINATING

FREEZE ME

DAIRY FREE

GLUTEN FREE

USE GF SOY SAUCE

PER SERVING:
341 KCAL /15G CARBS

3 tbsp soy sauce – dark or light works
3 tbsp honey
2 garlic cloves, peeled and crushed
5cm (2in) piece of root ginger, peeled and finely grated
½ tsp sriracha sauce
8 bone-in chicken thighs, skin and all visible fat removed, about 1kg
1 tbsp sesame seeds (optional)

TO ACCOMPANY *(optional)*
50g uncooked basmati rice, cooked according to packet instructions (+ 173 kcal per serving)

The moreish marinade for these Honey Soy Chicken Thighs is inspired by some of our favourite Asian flavours. With only a few ingredients (including a couple you probably already have in the cupboard), you can whip up this simple midweek meal in under an hour. In fact, why not prepare your chicken in the morning and leave it to marinate until dinnertime? This gives all those sweet, salty, aromatic flavours time to work their magic!

Weekly Indulgence —————————————————

Add the soy sauce, honey, garlic, ginger and sriracha sauce to a small mixing bowl and stir to combine.

Place the chicken thighs in an ovenproof dish and pour over the honey and soy sauce mix. Cover with cling film and allow to marinate for at least 1 hour in the fridge.

Preheat the oven to 220°C (fan 200°C/gas mark 7) then pop the chicken thighs in the oven and cook for 15 minutes.

After 15 minutes, turn the chicken thighs over so that the meat doesn't dry out. Cook for a further 15 minutes.

Again, turn the chicken over and cook for another 15 minutes. The sauce on the chicken thighs should have reduced and started to become sticky.

If using the sesame seeds, add to a frying pan and heat over a medium heat for a few minutes until lightly golden. Leave to one side.

Remove from the oven and check that the chicken thighs are cooked through and that no pinkness remains. Sprinkle over the toasted sesame seeds and serve with your choice of accompaniment.

Serve with basmati rice or your choice of accompaniment.

USE DF CHEESES

**USE GF PASTA AND
STOCK CUBE**

CREAMY TARRAGON
CHICKEN PASTA

🕐 **10 MINS** 🍲 **35 MINS** ✕ **SERVES 4**

PER SERVING:

330 KCAL /39G CARBS

SPECIAL EQUIPMENT
**18 x 27cm (7 x 10½in)
ovenproof dish**

low-calorie cooking spray
½ onion, peeled and finely
   diced
3 garlic cloves, peeled and
   crushed
260g diced chicken breast
100g button mushrooms,
   thinly sliced
1 tsp Dijon mustard
1 chicken stock cube
150ml boiling water
200g dried pasta, any shape
   you prefer
2 tbsp fresh tarragon leaves,
   finely chopped
120g reduced-fat cream
   cheese
40g reduced-fat Cheddar
   cheese, finely grated
sea salt and freshly ground
   black pepper, to taste

When you need a tasty and simple-to-make midweek meal, you can always rely on a good old pasta bake. Despite the name, there's no cream in this recipe – instead, we've used reduced-fat cream cheese to make the rich, silky, tarragon-infused sauce. Mixed in with pasta and tender chicken pieces, topped with Cheddar cheese and browned under the grill until it's golden and bubbling, this is guaranteed to be a crowd-pleaser at dinnertime.

Everyday Light ──────────────────

Spray a large frying pan with low-calorie cooking spray and place over a medium heat. Add the onion and garlic and cook gently for 4 minutes, until beginning to soften.

Add the diced chicken and cook for 2–3 minutes, until lightly browned. Add the mushrooms and cook for 5 minutes.

Add the mustard and stock cube to the boiling water and stir until dissolved. Pour into the frying pan and simmer, uncovered, for 8 minutes.

While the chicken is simmering, cook the pasta in a saucepan of boiling water for 8–10 minutes, or according to the packet instructions. Drain well.

Remove the frying pan from the heat and stir in the tarragon and cream cheese until completely blended. Season with salt and pepper to taste. Add the cooked pasta and stir to combine. Preheat the grill.

Pour the mixture into the ovenproof dish and sprinkle over the grated cheese. Pop under the grill for 5 minutes, until the cheese has melted and is golden and bubbly.

VEGGIE

VEGAN
USE VEGAN
STOCK CUBE

FREEZE
ME

DAIRY
FREE

GLUTEN
FREE
USE GF STOCK
CUBE AND
HENDERSON'S
RELISH

BATCH
FRIENDLY

SPICY TOMATO SOUP

🕐 **5 MINS**   🍳 **20 MINS**   ✕ **SERVES 4**

PER SERVING:
116 KCAL /17G CARBS

SPECIAL EQUIPMENT
Stick blender

low-calorie cooking spray
1 large white onion, peeled
   and sliced
2 celery sticks, chopped
4 garlic cloves, peeled and
   crushed
2 x 400g tins chopped
   tomatoes
250ml vegetable stock
   (1 vegetable stock cube
   dissolved in 250ml boiling
   water)
2 tbsp tomato puree
2 tbsp Henderson's relish or
   Worcestershire sauce
1 tsp smoked paprika
1 tsp lemon juice
1 tsp Tabasco sauce (add
   more or less to taste)
sea salt and freshly ground
   black pepper, to taste
fresh basil leaves, to serve
   (optional)

Our Spicy Tomato Soup is based on the classic flavours of a Bloody Mary cocktail. Even if you're not a fan of the drink, you'll love the soup! This recipe is super quick and easy, and it can be made mostly from store-cupboard essentials, making it an ideal lunch dish. You can swap the Tabasco for any other hot sauce or even a little chilli powder if you'd prefer, and feel free to make it milder or spicier to suit your tastes!

Everyday Light ───────────────

Spray a large saucepan with low-calorie cooking spray and place over a medium heat. Add the onion, celery and garlic and fry gently for 10 minutes until the onion has softened.

Add the rest of the ingredients and simmer for another 10 minutes.

Blend with a stick blender until smooth and serve with basil if you like.

FREEZE ME

ENCHILADA MIX ONLY

GLUTEN FREE

USE GF ROLLS AND HENDERSON'S RELISH

ENCHILADA SLIDERS

 15 MINS   🗑 **25 MINS**   ✕ **SERVES 6**

SUPER SAVER · SUPER SAVER ·

PER SERVING:

341 KCAL / 45G CARBS

SPECIAL EQUIPMENT
18 x 27cm (7 x 10½in) ovenproof dish

1 medium skinless chicken breast
low-calorie cooking spray
½ red pepper, deseeded and diced
½ green pepper, deseeded and diced
½ yellow pepper, deseeded and diced
½ x 400g tin black beans, about 120g, drained and rinsed
½ tsp ground cumin
½ tsp onion granules
½ tsp smoked paprika
½ tsp chilli powder
½ x 400g tin chopped tomatoes, about 200g
200g passata
1 tsp Worcestershire sauce or Henderson's relish

TO ASSEMBLE
6 wholemeal rolls, cut in half
6 reduced-fat processed cheese slices
2 tbsp passata
1 tsp reduced-fat spread, melted
1 spring onion, thinly sliced
5g reduced-fat Cheddar, finely grated

TO ACCOMPANY *(optional)*
Homemade Oven Chips (from the Pinch of Nom website, + 96 kcal per serving)

Once you try our fuss-free Enchilada Sliders, you might not go back to burgers in a hurry! An effortless blend of fiesta-worthy flavours, we can't think of a better place to give leftover peppers a new lease of life. The secret is in the showstopping filling: pulled chicken bubbles away in a tomatoey mixture of herbs, black beans and spices until it's too tasty to miss. Stack your sliders and grill until they're golden and crisp with a cheesy crunch.

Weekly Indulgence ——————————————

Add the chicken breast to a saucepan and cover with boiling water. Cook over a medium heat for 20 minutes. Remove and shred the chicken with two forks.

While the chicken is cooking, spray a frying pan with low-calorie cooking spray and place over a medium heat. Add the peppers and fry for 3 minutes.

Add the black beans and fry for another 2 minutes, until they are beginning to pop. Add the cumin, onion granules, smoked paprika and chilli powder and stir to coat the vegetables.

Pour in the chopped tomatoes, passata and Worcestershire sauce or Henderson's relish. Lower the heat and allow to simmer for 4 minutes until reduced slightly. Add the shredded chicken breast and stir to coat. Preheat the grill.

Place the bottom halves of the wholemeal rolls in the ovenproof dish and spoon on the enchilada mixture. Top each slider with a slice of cheese and pop under the grill for 2 minutes until melted.

Add a little of the passata to the inside of each wholemeal roll top and place on top of the enchilada mix.

Brush a little of the reduced-fat spread onto each roll and sprinkle over the spring onion and grated cheese. Pop back under the grill for a minute until the cheese is melted.

Serve with Homemade Oven Chips, or your choice of accompaniment.

SPINACH *and* PARMESAN ORZO

🕐 **5 MINS**   🗑 **16 MINS**   ✗ **SERVES 4**

PER SERVING:
253 KCAL / 39G CARBS

low-calorie cooking spray
1 onion, peeled and finely diced
2 garlic cloves, peeled and crushed
650ml vegetable stock (1 vegetable stock cube dissolved in 650ml boiling water)
50g reduced-fat cream cheese
200g orzo
30g Parmesan cheese, finely grated
75g baby spinach
freshly ground black pepper, to taste

We've used our favourite pasta shape to make this rich, filling, meat-free Spinach and Parmesan Orzo. Perfect for lunch or dinner, the tiny rice-shaped pasta pieces cook down until you have an indulgent, risotto-like dish, with a creamy, cheesy sauce. Simmer until the orzo is tender, while still having a 'bite' to it, so you've got a bit of texture. Finish with grated Parmesan and a sprinkling of black pepper and that's dinner sorted!

Everyday Light ―――――――――――――――

Spray a saucepan with low-calorie cooking spray and place over a medium heat. Add the onion and cook for 5 minutes, until soft.

Add the garlic and cook for another minute. Pour the vegetable stock into the pan along with the cream cheese and stir until the cheese has melted.

Add the orzo and bring to a simmer. Turn the heat down to low and cook for 12–15 minutes, stirring occasionally. When cooked, the pasta should be tender but with a 'bite' and most of the liquid will be absorbed, with a little remaining as a creamy sauce. Add a little more water if you need to.

Add the Parmesan and spinach and stir for about a minute, until the spinach wilts. Season with black pepper and serve!

VEGAN

FREEZE ME

CURRY SAUCE ONLY

DAIRY FREE

GLUTEN FREE

USE GF PANKO BREADCRUMBS, STOCK CUBE AND SOY SAUCE

VEGAN KATSU CURRY

🕐 **20 MINS**   🍲 **1 HR**   ✕ **SERVES 4**

PER SERVING:
283 KCAL / 26G CARBS

SPECIAL EQUIPMENT
Stick blender or food processor

low-calorie cooking spray
1 tbsp coconut dairy-free milk alternative
400g block of firm tofu, well drained
40g panko breadcrumbs

FOR THE CURRY SAUCE
1 onion, peeled and roughly chopped
2 garlic cloves, peeled and crushed
3 medium carrots, peeled and cut into 1cm (½in) dice
1 small potato, about 115g, peeled and cut into 1cm (½in) dice
1 tbsp garlic granules
1½ tsp onion granules
1½ tsp garam masala
1 tbsp mild curry powder
400ml vegetable stock (1 vegetable stock cube dissolved in 400ml boiling water)
1 tbsp dark soy sauce
1 tbsp white granulated sweetener
sea salt and freshly ground black pepper, to taste

List continues over the page ...

This curry is brimming with so much flavour, you'll never miss the meat. To keep things vegan friendly and lower in calories, we've swapped out chicken for crispy tofu, coated in light panko breadcrumbs. Rich with veggies, spices and just the right level of sweetness, it's tough to believe these Japanese-inspired flavours are slimming friendly. You're guaranteed to want the moreish katsu-style crunch again, so do yourself a favour and save extra sauce for another day!

Weekly Indulgence

Line a baking tray with foil and spray well with low-calorie cooking spray. Use to grease the tray thoroughly all over.

To make the curry sauce, spray a medium saucepan with low-calorie cooking spray and place over a medium heat. Add the onion and fry for 5 minutes until slightly softened, stirring occasionally. Add the garlic and cook for a further 1–2 minutes.

Add the carrots, potato, garlic granules, onion granules, garam masala, curry powder, vegetable stock, soy sauce and sweetener. Stir well. Lower the heat, cover and simmer for 20–25 minutes, stirring occasionally, until the vegetables are soft.

While the curry sauce is cooking, prepare the tofu. Pour the coconut dairy-free milk alternative into a shallow bowl and place the panko breadcrumbs on a plate. Season the breadcrumbs with salt and black pepper.

Preheat the oven to 220°C (fan 200°C/gas mark 7).

Place the well-drained block of tofu on a chopping board. Use kitchen towel to pat all sides of the tofu dry, removing as much excess water as possible. You will need to use several sheets of kitchen towel to do this.

Using a large, sharp knife, slice through the tofu block horizontally and make two rectangles about 2cm (¾in) in thickness. Cut each rectangle across diagonally to make two triangles. You should now have a total of four triangles about 2cm (¾in) in thickness.

TO GARNISH
lime slices
carrot strips
spring onion slices
coriander sprigs

TO ACCOMPANY *(optional)*
50g uncooked basmati rice,
  cooked according to packet
  instructions (+ 173 kcal per
  serving)

Dip one triangle in the coconut dairy-free milk alternative and turn carefully to coat all sides thoroughly. Place in the panko breadcrumbs and coat all sides, pressing the breadcrumbs on lightly. Place on the prepared baking tray and repeat with the remaining three tofu triangles.

Spray the top and sides of the breadcrumbed tofu with low-calorie cooking spray. Place in the preheated oven for 20–25 minutes until crisp and golden.

Once the curry sauce has finished cooking, blitz in the saucepan using a stick blender until really smooth. If the sauce is too thick, add a little water to thin it down. You could also use a food processor to blitz the sauce until smooth, and then return the sauce to the saucepan to keep warm.

When the breadcrumbed tofu has finished cooking, remove from the oven and use a large serrated knife to slice each piece across widthways into four or five slices.

Serve the sliced tofu with the curry sauce and basmati rice or accompaniment of your choice. Garnish each serving with a lime slice, carrot strips, spring onion slices and a sprig of coriander.

 TIP: You can choose what type of curry powder to use depending on your taste. We used mild, but you could choose to use medium or hot curry powder.

STICKY HARISSA *and* ORANGE CHICKEN

🕐 **10 MINS**   🍲 **30 MINS**   ✕ **SERVES 4**

PER SERVING:
394 KCAL /26G CARBS

FOR THE CHICKEN
2 tbsp no-added-sugar
 marmalade
1 tbsp harissa paste
1 garlic clove, peeled and
 crushed
grated zest of 1 orange
juice of ½ orange, about
 50ml
8 skinless boneless chicken
 thighs, about 1kg in total

FOR THE COUSCOUS
100g couscous
4g fresh mint, chopped
juice of ½ orange, about
 50ml
100ml boiling water
sea salt and freshly ground
 black pepper, to taste

Sweet and spicy, the sticky citrus glaze is the key to this easy recipe. You might not think to use marmalade in a marinade, but it really works! Combined with the smoky heat of the harissa paste, it transforms this simple dish into something that tastes really special. We love to use chicken thighs for this recipe – they're more succulent than chicken breast, and more budget friendly too! Prepare your chicken in advance and leave it to marinate in the fridge if you want an even deeper flavour.

Everyday Light ────────────────────

Preheat the oven to 220°C (fan 200°C/gas mark 7).

Add the marmalade, harissa, garlic, orange zest and orange juice to a small mixing bowl. Stir until combined.

Lay the chicken thighs out in an ovenproof dish. Pour over half the marmalade and harissa mixture, turn them over and pour the rest of the mixture over the other side of the thighs. Place the dish in the oven and cook for 20 minutes.

After 20 minutes spoon any of the harissa mixture from the bottom of the dish back over the thighs and cook for a further 10 minutes.

While the chicken thighs are cooking, add the couscous to a bowl. Add the mint and pour over the orange juice and boiling water. Stir and cover the bowl, and allow it to sit for 10 minutes until the water is absorbed. Fluff up the couscous with a fork and season with salt and pepper to taste.

Check that the chicken thighs are cooked through and that no pinkness remains. Remove from the oven and serve with the couscous.

TIP: Once you've opened the harissa paste it can be kept in the fridge for up to 1 month ready for next time!

FREEZE ME

DAIRY FREE

GLUTEN FREE

USE GF STOCK CUBE

BATCH FRIENDLY

BAKED BEAN CHILLI

🕐 **15 MINS**   🍲 **45 MINS**   ✕ **SERVES 4**

PER SERVING:
282 KCAL / 31G CARBS

low-calorie cooking spray
1 large onion, peeled and diced
250g 5%-fat minced beef
2 mixed peppers, deseeded and diced
1 carrot, peeled and cut into 1cm (½in) dice
1 tbsp chilli powder (mild or hot, depending on your preference)
2 tsp garlic granules
1 tsp ground cumin
1 x 400g tin chopped tomatoes
300ml beef stock (1 beef stock cube dissolved in 300ml boiling water)
1 x 420g tin baked beans, reduced sugar and salt

TO ACCOMPANY
50g uncooked basmati rice, cooked according to packet instructions (+ 173 kcal per serving)

A dreamy dish that will feed the whole family, this Baked Bean Chilli is well worth an hour of your time. Prepared with simple store-cupboard staples, we've also made the most of the basics from your spice rack. Aside from chilli-infused mince and fresh veggies, we've turned the flavours up a notch with a surprise ingredient: baked beans! A budget-friendly way to add fresh texture and richness for fewer calories, don't knock it until you've tried it (and loved it!).

Weekly Indulgence ───────────

Spray a large pan with low-calorie cooking spray and place over a medium heat. Add the onion and sauté for 5 minutes until softened.

Add the mince and, stirring with a wooden spoon to break up any lumps, continue to cook for 3–4 minutes until browned. Add the peppers, carrot, chilli powder, garlic granules and cumin and stir well.

Stir in the chopped tomatoes and stock and bring to the boil.

Turn the heat down to a simmer and cook uncovered for 30 minutes, stirring occasionally.

Add the baked beans and continue cooking for 5 minutes until heated through. Serve with the basmati rice.

CREAMY BEEF *and* POTATO PIE

🕐 **25 MINS**   🍲 **2 HRS**   ✕ **SERVES 6**

PER SERVING:
327 KCAL / 37G CARBS

SPECIAL EQUIPMENT
18 x 27cm (7 x 10½in) ovenproof dish

low-calorie cooking spray
500g 5%-fat minced beef
1 onion, peeled and diced
4 garlic cloves, peeled and crushed
2 medium carrots, peeled and cut into small dice
1 medium courgette, cut into small dice
1 medium red pepper, deseeded and cut into small dice
1 medium green pepper, deseeded and cut into small dice
1 x 400g tin chopped tomatoes
175ml skimmed milk
250ml beef stock (1 beef stock cube dissolved in 250ml boiling water)
1 white wine stock pot
handful of fresh basil, chopped
90g reduced-fat cream cheese
sea salt and freshly ground black pepper, to taste

FOR THE TOP
800g potatoes, peeled and cut into large chunks
35ml chicken stock (¼ chicken stock cube dissolved in 35ml boiling water)
1 tsp garlic granules
25g reduced-fat cream cheese

If you're already a fan of the Creamy Bolognese recipe from our website, you're sure to love this hearty, potato-topped pie. The rich, meaty filling is packed with lots of extra veggies, making this a great alternative to a family Sunday dinner. Our smooth, creamy, garlicky mash is the perfect finishing touch; spoon it on top and bake it in the oven until the whole thing is golden brown and piping hot all the way through.

Everyday Light ──────────────

Spray a large saucepan with low-calorie cooking spray and place over a medium heat. Add the minced beef and brown for 5–6 minutes, stirring with a wooden spoon to break up any lumps.

Add the onion and garlic and continue to cook for another 3–4 minutes. Add the carrots, courgette and peppers, then stir in the tinned tomatoes.

Stir in the milk, beef stock and white wine stock pot (no need to dissolve this in water first, it will dissolve in the pan). Bring to the boil, then reduce the heat to a gentle simmer. Cover and cook for 40 minutes, stirring occasionally.

After 40 minutes, remove the lid and stir in the basil. Continue cooking, uncovered, for another 35–40 minutes. During this time the sauce should reduce until the mixture is thick and most of the liquid has gone. If the mixture is still too wet, continue to simmer, uncovered, until thickened and reduced.

When cooked, stir in the cream cheese until evenly blended and taste. Season with salt and black pepper, if needed. Place the mixture into the ovenproof dish and spread out evenly. Preheat the oven to 200°C (fan 180°C/gas mark 6).

While the beef mixture is cooking, cook the potatoes. Place the potatoes in a large saucepan with enough cold water to cover. Cover with a lid and place over a high heat. Bring to the boil, then lower the heat and simmer for 20 minutes or until the potatoes are soft when tested with a sharp knife.

Drain the potatoes well and return to the saucepan. Mash until smooth. Stir in the chicken stock, garlic granules and

TIPS: If batch cooking, cool as quickly as possible, divide into individual servings and freeze at once. You could use minced pork or turkey instead of beef, if you prefer.

cream cheese. Season with salt and black pepper to taste. Spoon the potato mixture over the beef filling and spread out to cover completely. Use a fork to texture the top if wished.

Set on a baking tray and place in the preheated oven for 25 minutes or until golden on top and piping hot throughout.

FREEZE ME

DAIRY FREE

USE DF CHEESE

GLUTEN FREE

USE GF STOCK CUBES

BATCH FRIENDLY

CHICKEN, BACON *and* LEEK SOUP

SUPER SAVER · SUPER SAVER

🕐 **15 MINS**   🍲 **45 MINS**   ✕ **SERVES 4**

PER SERVING:
169 KCAL / 19G CARBS

SPECIAL EQUIPMENT
Food processor or stick blender

low-calorie cooking spray

1 onion, peeled and chopped

2 medium leeks, trimmed and chopped

2 skinless boneless chicken thighs (visible fat removed), about 75g each

2 unsmoked bacon medallions, cut into 1cm (½in) dice

2 medium potatoes, about 150g each, peeled and cut into 2cm (¾in) chunks

1 litre chicken stock (2 very low-salt chicken stock cubes dissolved in 1 litre boiling water)

¼ tsp mustard powder

½ tsp dried thyme

½ tsp dried parsley

25g reduced-fat cream cheese

sea salt and freshly ground black pepper, to taste

TO ACCOMPANY *(optional)*
60g crusty wholemeal bread roll (+ 144 kcal per serving)

TIP: We used chicken thighs as we think they have a better flavour than breasts, but you could use an equal amount of chicken breast if you prefer.

If you've ever tried our Chicken, Bacon and Leek Cottage Pie recipe, you'll know this is a winning flavour combination. With potatoes and reduced-fat cream cheese blended in, this soup is properly hearty, creamy and warming. Put your feet up with a bowlful for lunch and we guarantee you won't be disappointed!

Everyday Light

Spray a large saucepan with low-calorie cooking spray and place over a medium heat. Add the onion and leeks and cook for 5 minutes until beginning to soften.

Add the whole chicken thighs, bacon, potatoes, chicken stock, mustard powder, thyme and parsley. Bring to the boil, then lower the heat, cover with a lid and simmer for 35–40 minutes, until the potato is soft, and the chicken is cooked through and shows no sign of pinkness.

Remove the cooked chicken thighs and place on a plate. Use two forks to finely shred and set aside.

Blitz the soup until smooth in a food processor or using a stick blender. You may need to do this in two batches depending on the size of your food processor. Return the smooth soup to the saucepan and stir in the cream cheese until completely blended.

Stir in the shredded chicken and season to taste with salt and black pepper, if needed. Serve with a crusty wholemeal roll or other accompaniment of choice.

FREEZE
ME

DAIRY
FREE

GLUTEN
FREE

USE GF SOY
SAUCE

PINEAPPLE PORK

🕐 **15 MINS***   🗑 **8 MINS**   ✗ **SERVES 4**

*PLUS OVERNIGHT MARINATING

PER SERVING:

387 KCAL /26G CARBS

FOR THE PORK

2 tbsp soy sauce – dark or light works well

2 tbsp reduced-sugar ketchup

2 tbsp white granulated sweetener

½ tsp ground ginger

½ tsp Chinese 5-spice

2 garlic cloves, peeled and crushed

2 tbsp orange juice

4 pork loin steaks, approx. 120g per loin steak, all visible fat removed

4 rings of fresh pineapple, approx. 300g

FOR THE SALAD

100g pak choi, thinly sliced

100g red cabbage, thinly sliced

1 carrot, peeled and grated

50g sugar snap peas, cut in half

1 spring onion, thinly sliced

1 tbsp orange juice

1 tbsp lime juice

1 tbsp rice wine vinegar

½ tsp soy sauce

½ tsp white granulated sweetener

¼ tsp sriracha sauce

A match made in heaven, you won't be able to resist our oh-so-juicy Pineapple Pork. We've saved on pennies (and calories!) by coating our steaks in a sweet yet sticky glaze and leaving the flavours to marinate overnight. Served alongside a fresh, crunchy rainbow salad, every bite is bursting with flavour that'll brighten up dinnertime in an instant! Bound to be a hit with the whole family, we love how easy it is to put together this impressive dish.

Everyday Light ────────────────────

In a small bowl combine the soy sauce, ketchup, sweetener, ginger, Chinese 5-spice, garlic and orange juice. Add the pork loin steaks and pineapple and turn to coat. Cover and leave to marinate in the fridge overnight.

When the pork has marinated, make the salad. Place the pak choi, red cabbage, carrot, sugar snap peas and spring onion in a bowl. Combine the orange juice, lime juice, rice wine vinegar, soy sauce, sweetener and sriracha in a small bowl and pour over the salad. Toss to coat and leave to one side while you cook the pork.

Preheat the grill and, reserving the marinade, place the pork steaks and pineapple in a baking tray. Put under the grill for 4 minutes, then turn and cook for another 4 minutes.

Pour the reserved marinade into a small saucepan and bring to the boil. Lower the heat and simmer slowly until thickened to a glaze.

Serve each pork steak with a slice of pineapple and a drizzle of the glaze and salad.

VEGGIE

USE VEGGIE
HARD CHEESE

VEGAN

USE VEGAN
CHEESES

FREEZE
ME

SAUCE ONLY

DAIRY
FREE

USE DF
CHEESES

GLUTEN
FREE

USE GF PASTA

ROASTED BUTTERNUT SQUASH PASTA

🕐 **15 MINS** 🍲 **1 HR** ✕ **SERVES 4**

PER SERVING:
316 KCAL /48G CARBS

SPECIAL EQUIPMENT
Food processor

350g butternut squash,
  peeled and cut into chunks
1 red onion, peeled and cut
  into quarters
4 garlic cloves, peeled
low-calorie cooking spray
1 tsp dried thyme
1 tsp dried sage
1 tsp mild chilli powder
50ml boiling water
3 tbsp reduced-fat cream
  cheese
200g dried spaghetti
50g spinach, roughly
  chopped
20g Parmesan cheese, finely
  grated
sea salt and freshly ground
  black pepper, to taste

You'd never guess this creamy pasta dish is low in calories and good for you too! Forget shop-bought sauces, our homemade version is tastier, thriftier and packed with hidden vegetables. We've roasted butternut squash with fresh garlic and store-cupboard herbs, before adding reduced-fat cream cheese and blending it into a silky sauce. It's a sure-fire way to transform humble spaghetti into proper comfort food.

Everyday Light ──────────────────

Preheat the oven to 200°C (fan 180°C/gas mark 6).

Add the butternut squash, red onion and garlic cloves to a baking tray and spray with low-calorie cooking spray.

Sprinkle over the thyme, sage and chilli powder and toss to coat. Place in the oven for 50 minutes, shaking the tray halfway through.

Once the butternut squash is soft and turning golden around the edges, remove the tray from the oven. Tip the vegetables into a food processor, add the water and blitz until smooth. Add the cream cheese and blitz again until combined. Season to taste with salt and black pepper.

Fill a saucepan with water, bring to the boil, add the spaghetti and cook according to the packet instructions (ours took 10 minutes). Just before draining the spaghetti, add the spinach to the pan to allow it to wilt for a minute or so.

Drain the spaghetti and spinach, saving some of the pasta water. Add the spaghetti back to the pan, pour over the butternut squash mixture and stir to coat. Add a splash of the pasta water a little at a time to get the desired consistency to coat the spaghetti.

Sprinkle over the Parmesan cheese and serve!

TOMATO *and* CARAMELIZED ONION TARTS

🕐 **10 MINS**   🗑 **30 MINS**   🗡 **SERVES 8**

VEGGIE

VEGAN

USE VEGAN
CHEESE AND DF
MILK

FREEZE
ME

DAIRY
FREE

USE DF CHEESE
AND MILK

GLUTEN
FREE

USE GF PASTRY

PER TART:
220 KCAL /24G CARBS

low-calorie cooking spray
3 onions, peeled and thinly
  sliced
2 tsp balsamic vinegar
½ tsp garlic granules
320g ready-rolled light puff
  pastry sheet, about 35 x
  23cm (14 x 9in)
80g reduced-fat mature
  Cheddar, finely grated
8 slices of tomato, halved
1 tsp skimmed milk, for
  brushing
sea salt and freshly ground
  black pepper, to taste

TO ACCOMPANY *(optional)*
Homemade Oven Chips (from
  the Pinch of Nom website,
  + 96 kcal per serving)

Topped with sweet, soft, caramelized onions and plenty of cheese, these easy puff pastry tarts truly are a thing of beauty. They only take 10 minutes to prepare, and then you can let your oven do the rest of the work. When they're ready, you'll be biting into layers of flaky puff pastry, melt-in-the-mouth onions, sweet tomato and creamy, melted cheese. We can't think of anything we'd rather make for lunch today!

Everyday Light

Preheat the oven to 220°C (fan 200°C/gas mark 7). Spray a large frying pan with low-calorie cooking spray and place over a medium-low heat. Add the onions and cook slowly for about 15 minutes, stirring occasionally, until softened, golden and caramelized.

Stir in the balsamic vinegar and garlic granules and season to taste with salt and black pepper. When the balsamic vinegar has evaporated, remove from the heat and allow to cool slightly.

Unroll the pastry sheet and place it on a large baking tray, still on the greaseproof paper packaging sheet. Cut the pastry into eight rectangles, each about 8 x 12cm (3 x 4½in). Carefully space the pastry rectangles out, leaving small gaps between each.

Use a small, sharp knife to lightly score a line around each pastry rectangle, about 1cm (½in) in from the edge. Take care not to cut right through the pastry. Use a fork to prick the centre of each pastry rectangle, but not the edges.

Divide half the cheese between the pastry rectangles. Place in the centre and spread out evenly, leaving the edges free of cheese.

Divide the caramelized onions into eight portions and place on top of the cheese. Spread out evenly to make a thick layer, leaving the edges free of onions.

Use the remaining cheese to sprinkle over the onions. Place a halved tomato slice on top of each tart.

Brush the edges of the tarts with milk and place in the preheated oven for 15 minutes, or until crisp and golden brown.

Serve alone, with Homemade Oven Chips or other accompaniment of your choice.

TIPS: You will have a thick layer of onions on the tarts, this will reduce down after baking in the oven. We used brown onions, but you could try using red onions instead. Get creative and add your own combinations of ingredients on these crisp tarts.

VEGGIE
USE VEGGIE CHEESE

VEGAN
USE VEGAN CHEESE AND DF MILK

FREEZE ME

DAIRY FREE
USE DF CHEESE AND MILK

GLUTEN FREE
USE GF PASTA

BATCH FRIENDLY

CURRIED MACARONI CHEESE

🕐 **15 MINS**   🍲 **35 MINS**   ✕ **SERVES 4**

PER SERVING:
430 KCAL / 56G CARBS

SPECIAL EQUIPMENT
18 x 27cm (7 x 10½in) ovenproof dish

200g dried macaroni

FOR THE CURRIED CHEESE SAUCE
low-calorie cooking spray
1 onion, peeled and finely chopped
1 medium green pepper, deseeded and cut into 1cm (½in) dice
1 medium red pepper, deseeded and cut into 1cm (½in) dice
3 garlic cloves, peeled and crushed
2cm (¾in) piece of root ginger, peeled and grated
1 red chilli, deseeded and finely chopped
1 tbsp mild curry powder
1 tbsp garam masala
1 tsp ground cumin
500ml skimmed milk
2 tbsp cornflour
2 tbsp cold water
140g reduced-fat Cheddar, finely grated
sea salt, to taste

FOR THE TOP
20g reduced-fat Cheddar, finely grated
a few thin slices of red chilli, to garnish (optional)

We've given Mac and Cheese a spicy makeover, and we can't wait for you to try it! With curry powder and red chillies mixed into the cheese sauce, this dish has a good kick to it. We think the fiery heat works well, balanced with the creamy Cheddar, but you can make this recipe milder if you prefer (just leave out the red chillies). This is proper comfort food – simple to make and ready to eat in well under an hour.

Weekly Indulgence

Place the macaroni in a large saucepan of boiling water and cook for about 8 minutes or until 'al dente'. Take care not to overcook. Drain well, return to the saucepan, cover and set aside. Preheat the oven to 200°C (fan 180°C/gas mark 6).

Spray a medium saucepan with low-calorie cooking spray and place over a medium heat. Add the onion and peppers and cook for 5 minutes, until starting to soften.

Add the garlic, ginger and chilli and cook for a further 5 minutes.

Lower the heat and stir in the curry powder, garam masala and cumin. Cook gently for 1–2 minutes.

Add the milk to the mixture in the saucepan, stirring until well blended. In a small bowl, mix the cornflour and water until smooth. Pour the cornflour mixture into the saucepan and simmer, stirring constantly, over a medium heat for 4–5 minutes until thickened. Remove from the heat and stir in the cheese until melted. Season with salt to taste.

Pour the curried cheese sauce into the cooked macaroni in the large saucepan. Stir until combined, then transfer into the ovenproof dish. Spread out evenly and sprinkle the 20g Cheddar over the top. Scatter a few red chilli slices over the cheese, if you like, and place in the preheated oven for 15–20 minutes, until bubbling and golden. Serve.

TIPS: Take care not to overcook the pasta; after boiling it needs to still have some 'bite' as it will be cooked further in the oven. We seasoned with salt only; we felt it didn't need black pepper.

BAKED TERIYAKI TOFU

🕐 **5 MINS***   🍲 **35 MINS**   ✕ **SERVES 4**

*PLUS TOFU-PRESSING TIME

PER SERVING:
194 KCAL / 19G CARBS

300g firm tofu
low-calorie cooking spray
80g broccoli, cut into bite-
   sized florets
80g mangetout, sliced in half
   lengthways
80g baby corn, sliced into
   1cm (½in)-thick slices
80g red pepper, deseeded
   and sliced
2 spring onions, thinly sliced

FOR THE TERIYAKI SAUCE
100ml cold water
3 tbsp dark soy sauce
2 tbsp white granulated
   sweetener
1 garlic clove, peeled and
   crushed
3cm (1¼in) piece of root
   ginger, peeled and finely
   grated
½ tbsp rice vinegar
1 tsp lime juice
¼ tsp onion granules
2 tsp cornflour

TIP: Pressing the moisture out of tofu results in a firmer and tastier tofu so don't skip this step.

Bursting with colour and vibrant flavour, it's impossible to make a dull dinner with our vegan-friendly Baked Teriyaki Tofu. We always press our tofu before we oven-bake it, to make sure it stays firm and the sweet yet tangy homemade teriyaki coating really soaks in. While we've added a medley of broccoli, mangetout, peppers and baby corn to our pan, there's nothing to stop you enjoying a different mix of crunchy stir-fried veggies each time!

Everyday Light ————————————————

Place a few layers of kitchen towel or clean cloth on the work surface. Put the tofu block on top and then cover with another layer of kitchen towel or another cloth. Place a weight on top of the tofu block; cookbooks work great, or a heavy pan. Leave for 30 minutes. The weight will squeeze out the moisture from the tofu – you may need to change the kitchen towel if it becomes too wet.

Preheat the oven to 210°C (fan 190°C/gas mark 6).

To make the teriyaki sauce, combine the water, soy sauce, sweetener, garlic, ginger, rice vinegar, lime juice and onion granules in a medium saucepan. Set the saucepan on a medium heat and bring to a low simmer. Cook for 5–6 minutes until beginning to thicken.

Combine the cornflour with 2 teaspoons of cold water in a small bowl and mix until smooth. Add to the pan and stir. Cook for another minute until the sauce has thickened and leave to one side.

Once you have pressed your tofu, cut roughly into 1cm (½in) squares and place in an ovenproof dish. Reserve 3 tablespoons of the teriyaki sauce then pour the rest over the tofu and toss to coat. Pop into the oven and cook for 20 minutes.

Spray a frying pan with low-calorie cooking spray and place over a medium heat. Add the broccoli, mangetout, baby corn and pepper and stir-fry for 4 minutes. The vegetables should be starting to colour and getting slightly charred around the edges but still be quite firm.

Remove the tofu from the oven and add the stir-fried vegetables. Toss to coat the vegetables in the sauce and put back into the oven for 10 minutes.

Sprinkle with the sliced spring onion, drizzle over the reserved teriyaki sauce and serve.

FREEZE ME

SAUCE ONLY

DAIRY FREE

USE DF CHEESE

GLUTEN FREE

USE GF STOCK CUBES AND SPAGHETTI

BATCH FRIENDLY

KEEMA SPAGHETTI

 15 MINS   **30 MINS**   ✕ **SERVES 6**

PER SERVING:
331 KCAL /44G CARBS

low-calorie cooking spray
400g 5%-fat minced beef
1 onion, peeled and diced
1 medium red pepper,
    deseeded and diced
1 medium green pepper,
    deseeded and diced
2 medium carrots, peeled
    and diced
1cm (½in) piece of root
    ginger, peeled and grated
2 tsp garlic granules
2 tbsp curry powder
3 tbsp tomato puree
450ml beef stock (2 beef
    stock cubes dissolved in
    450ml boiling water)
juice of ½ lemon
150g frozen peas
sea salt and freshly ground
    black pepper, to taste
300g dried spaghetti

Spice up dinnertime with this family-friendly Keema Spaghetti. We like to think of it as our Indian-inspired twist on Spaghetti Bolognese, and chances are you've already got most of the ingredients in your store cupboard! We've simmered low-fat minced beef in a garlicky, curried stock until it's brimming with keema-style flavour. Ready in 45 minutes, we're betting fussy eaters won't be able to resist twirling this tasty spaghetti round their fork (even with onions, peppers, carrots and peas in the mix!).

Everyday Light ―――――――――――――――――――

Spray a large saucepan with low-calorie cooking spray and place over a medium-high heat. Add the mince and, stirring with a wooden spoon to break up any lumps. brown on all sides for 4–5 minutes.

Add the onion, peppers and carrots and continue cooking for another 3–4 minutes.

Add the ginger, garlic granules and curry powder. Stir well, then add the tomato puree. Pour in the beef stock, squeeze in the lemon juice, stir well and bring to the boil.

Reduce the heat to low and allow to simmer, uncovered, for 20 minutes. The sauce should reduce and thicken. If you think it's a bit runny, cook it for a little longer. Stir in the frozen peas and cook for 1–2 minutes. Taste and season with salt and black pepper if needed.

While the mince is cooking, place a large saucepan of water over a high heat. Cover and bring to the boil. Add the spaghetti and cook for about 8–10 minutes or according to the packet instructions, until tender. Drain well and return to the saucepan.

Add the keema mixture to the spaghetti in the saucepan and stir to combine. Serve at once.

FREEZE ME

DAIRY FREE

GLUTEN FREE

USE HENDERSON'S RELISH

BATCH FRIENDLY

MIX-IT-UP MINCE

 🕐 **20 MINS** 🍲 **VARIABLE** (SEE BELOW) ✕ **SERVES 8**

PER SERVING:
157 KCAL / 13G CARBS

low-calorie cooking spray
500g 5%-fat minced beef
2 onions, peeled and finely diced
4 garlic cloves, peeled and crushed
1 medium red pepper, deseeded and finely diced
1 medium green pepper, deseeded and finely diced
2 large carrots, peeled and finely diced
2 celery sticks, finely diced
2 medium courgettes, finely diced
150g white mushrooms, finely chopped
1 x 400g tin chopped tomatoes
1 tbsp tomato puree
2 rich beef stock pots
2 tbsp Worcestershire sauce or Henderson's relish
2 tsp dried mixed herbs
sea salt and freshly ground black pepper, to taste

TO ACCOMPANY *(optional)*
50g uncooked basmati rice, cooked according to packet instructions (+ 173 kcal per serving)

TIPS: Prepare all the vegetables before starting the recipe – then you'll be organized and ready for each step! You can save your Mix-It-Up Mince in the fridge or freezer in batches to make a tasty dish on another day.

With our thrifty Mix-It-Up Mince, you can transform humble minced beef and inexpensive veggies into the savoury base for countless home-cooked meals. It works really well as a filling for potato-topped pies and pastry-wrapped bakes, or serve it with your favourite faff-free accompaniment (pasta, rice, chips – anything goes!). Whether you rustle it up on the hob and stick it in the oven, leave it to simmer in the slow cooker or throw it together in a hurry in the electric pressure cooker this one's ready when you want it, how you want it!

Everyday Light ───────────────────

OVEN METHOD
🍲 **1 HR 40 MINS**

Preheat the oven to 180°C (fan 160°C/gas mark 4). Spray a large, deep frying pan with low-calorie cooking spray and place over a medium heat. Add the minced beef and cook for 4–5 minutes. stirring with a wooden spoon to break up any lumps, until browned on all sides.

Add the onions, garlic, peppers, carrots and celery and cook for a further 4–5 minutes, stirring occasionally. Transfer the mixture to a large casserole dish and add the courgettes, mushrooms, chopped tomatoes, tomato puree, stock pots, Worcestershire sauce or Henderson's relish and mixed herbs. Stir well until the stock pots have dissolved.

Cover with a tightly-fitting lid and place in the oven for 1¼–1½ hours, stirring halfway through, until the mixture is thick and the vegetables are soft. Check occasionally to make sure the mixture isn't drying out and add a little water, if needed. If the mixture is not thick enough at the end of cooking, remove the lid and continue cooking for a little longer until reduced and thickened.

Taste and season with salt and black pepper, if needed. Serve with basmati rice or your choice of accompaniment.

SLOW-COOKER METHOD
🍲 5 HRS 10 MINS

SPECIAL EQUIPMENT
Slow cooker

Cook the minced beef, onions, garlic, peppers, carrots and celery in a large, deep frying pan, as explained on page 144. Transfer the mixture to the slow cooker and add the courgettes, mushrooms, chopped tomatoes, tomato puree, stock pots, Worcestershire sauce or Henderson's relish and mixed herbs. Stir well until the stock pots have dissolved.

Cover and cook on high for 5 hours until the mixture is thick and the vegetables are soft. If you think the mixture is not thick enough at the end of cooking, remove the lid and continue cooking for a further 30 minutes, until reduced and thickened.

Taste and season with salt and black pepper, if needed. Serve with basmati rice or your choice of accompaniment.

ELECTRIC PRESSURE-COOKER METHOD
🍲 40 MINS

SPECIAL EQUIPMENT
Electric pressure cooker

Spray the pressure-cooker pot with low-calorie cooking spray and set to 'sauté'. Add the minced beef and cook for 4–5 minutes. stirring with a wooden spoon to break up any lumps, until browned on all sides.

Add the onions, garlic, peppers, carrots and celery and cook for a further 4–5 minutes, stirring occasionally. Add the courgettes, mushrooms, chopped tomatoes, tomato puree, stock pots, Worcestershire sauce and mixed herbs. Stir well until the stock pots have dissolved.

Place the lid onto the pressure cooker and set the valve to 'sealing'. Select manual high pressure and set a time of 30 minutes. Once the pressure cooker has reached pressure, the timer will begin to count down. Once the timer has finished, set the valve to 'venting' to manually release pressure. The mixture should be thick and the vegetables soft. If you think the mixture is not thick enough, remove the lid and continue to sauté for a little longer, until reduced and thickened.

Taste and season with salt and black pepper, if needed. Serve with basmati rice or your choice of accompaniment.

VEGGIE

USE VEGGIE
ITALIAN HARD
CHEESE AND
HENDERSON'S
RELISH

FREEZE ME

DAIRY FREE

USE DF CHEESES

GLUTEN FREE

USE GF
PASTA AND
HENDERSON'S
RELISH

BATCH FRIENDLY

CREAMY TOMATO PASTA BAKE

🕐 **20 MINS**   🍲 **45 MINS**   ✗ **SERVES 4**

PER SERVING:
490 KCAL / 77G CARBS

SPECIAL EQUIPMENT
20 x 30cm (8 x 12in)
ovenproof dish

low-calorie cooking spray
500g cherry tomatoes,
    halved
sea salt and freshly ground
    black pepper, to taste
300g dried pasta twists
1 onion, peeled and chopped
4 garlic cloves, peeled and
    crushed
300g button mushrooms,
    thinly sliced
500g passata
200ml vegetable stock
    (½ vegetable stock cube
    dissolved in 200ml boiling
    water)
1 tsp dried oregano
2 tsp white granulated
    sweetener or caster sugar
2 tsp Worcestershire sauce or
    Henderson's relish
1 tbsp tomato puree
180g reduced-fat cream
    cheese
25g fresh basil leaves,
    stalks removed and leaves
    roughly torn
10g Parmesan cheese, finely
    grated, for the top

A good pasta bake is a thing of beauty, and shop-bought sauces have got nothing on this recipe. Without needing any fancy ingredients, we've built up layers of rich tomato flavours to create a family-friendly dinner that you'll want on repeat. We love how the roasted cherry tomatoes add a pop of sweetness that cuts right through the creamy sauce, with fresh basil and salty Parmesan to round off every bite of pasta perfection!

Weekly Indulgence

Preheat the oven to 220°C (fan 200°C/gas mark 7). Line a large baking tray with kitchen foil and spray with low-calorie cooking spray. Use it to thoroughly grease the foil.

Place the tomato halves on the greased foil, cut side up.

Spritz the tomatoes with a little low-calorie spray and season with salt and black pepper. Place in the preheated oven for 20 minutes, until softening and beginning to wrinkle around the edges. Remove from the oven and set aside. Lower the oven temperature to 200°C (fan 180°C/gas mark 6).

While the tomatoes are cooking, cook the pasta twists in a large saucepan of boiling water for 8–10 minutes, or according to the packet instructions. Cook until the pasta still has some 'bite', taking care not to overcook it. Drain well and set aside.

While the tomatoes and pasta are cooking, fry the onion. Spray a large frying pan with low-calorie cooking spray and place over a medium heat. Add the onion and fry for 5 minutes, until softening and golden.

Add the garlic and continue to cook for a further 1–2 minutes, stirring. Add the mushrooms and fry for 5 minutes, until the juices released from the mushrooms have evaporated.

Lower the heat and add the passata, stock, oregano, sweetener or sugar, Worcestershire sauce and tomato puree. Simmer, uncovered, for 5 minutes until slightly reduced and slightly thickened.

Remove the frying pan from the heat. Stir in the cream cheese and basil leaves until completely blended in, and the basil leaves are just wilting.

Stir in half of the roasted tomatoes and the cooked pasta, until evenly mixed. Transfer to the ovenproof dish and spread out evenly.

TIP: Take care not to overcook the pasta twists otherwise they may become mushy after baking. They need to have a little 'bite' after boiling.

Place the remaining roasted tomatoes on top and sprinkle with the Parmesan cheese. Put on a baking tray and place in the oven for about 15 minutes, until hot throughout and the cheese has melted on top. Serve.

Desserts

USING GRANULATED
SWEETENER WITH THE
SAME WEIGHT AND TEXTURE
AS SUGAR IS CRUCIAL TO
THE SUCCESS OF MANY
OF THESE RECIPES

BISCOFF BANANA BREAD

🕐 **10 MINS**   🍲 **40–45 MINS**   ✕ **SERVES 10**

PER SERVING:
262 KCAL / 33G CARBS

SPECIAL EQUIPMENT
450g loaf tin
Electric whisk

100g reduced-fat spread, plus a little extra for greasing
2 ripe medium bananas, peeled and mashed with a fork
30g caster sugar
30g white granulated sweetener
3 medium eggs
250g self-raising flour
50g fat-free Greek-style yoghurt
60g smooth Biscoff spread, plus 1 tsp for the top
10g white chocolate chips
10g milk chocolate chips

Bananas and Biscoff taste like they were always meant to go together. You can rely on this dreamy flavour combo to satisfy your sweet tooth, especially when it comes in the form of this irresistible teatime treat. The recipe is best made with sweet ripe or overripe bananas so use up any sorry-looking ones from the fruit bowl. It's delicious fresh from the oven, but don't forget you can also slice it up and freeze the individual portions for a snack emergency!

Weekly Indulgence ─────────────────

Preheat the oven to 200°C (fan 180°C/gas mark 6) and grease the loaf tin with a little reduced-fat spread. Line the base and sides of the tin with non-stick baking paper.

Add the mashed bananas, sugar, sweetener and reduced-fat spread to a large mixing bowl. Whisk with an electric whisk until light and fluffy. Add the eggs, flour and yoghurt and whisk again until combined and creamy.

In a small bowl, heat the smooth Biscoff spread in the microwave until just melted (or see Tip for melting without a microwave). Pour into the banana bread mixture and whisk again until combined.

Pour the mixture into the prepared tin, stopping when the mixture sits 1cm (½in) below the rim, then level the surface and sprinkle over both kinds of chocolate chips. Bake in the oven for 40–45 minutes until risen and golden brown. Insert a skewer into the centre of the loaf, it should come out clean.

Leave until cool to the touch, then remove the banana bread from the tin. Remove the lining paper and leave to cool completely on a cooling rack. Heat the 1 teaspoon of Biscoff spread in the microwave (or see Tip) until just melted. Drizzle over the top of the banana bread and serve.

TIP: If you don't have a microwave, melt the Biscoff spread by adding it to a small heatproof bowl. Place the bowl into a slightly larger bowl containing boiling water and stir for about 2 minutes until runny and smooth.

VEGGIE

FREEZE ME

GLUTEN FREE

WITHOUT THE
BISCUIT CRUMB

NEAPOLITAN ICE POPS

SUPER SAVER · SUPER SAVER ·

🕐 **20 MINS***   🗑 **NO-COOK**   ✕ **MAKES 6**

*PLUS FREEZING

PER SERVING:
84 KCAL /14G CARBS

SPECIAL EQUIPMENT
Food processor
6 ice lolly moulds

FOR THE CHOCOLATE LAYER
1 medium banana, peeled and sliced
2 tsp cocoa powder

FOR THE WHITE LAYER
1 medium banana, peeled and sliced

FOR THE STRAWBERRY LAYER
100g strawberries, stalks removed and fruit sliced
1 medium banana, peeled and sliced

FOR THE TOPPING
10g milk chocolate, broken into squares
2 Oreo biscuits, broken into crumbs

Chocolate, strawberry, banana . . . why choose one flavour when you can have them all? Inspired by the classic triple ice cream flavour, these Neapolitan Ice Pops are a great way to use up any bananas that are looking a little past their best. Blended and frozen, they turn into a creamy ice-cold treat – and we've made it even more delicious with a drizzle of melted chocolate and some biscuit crumbs sprinkled on top.

Everyday Light ———————————————————

For the chocolate layer, add the banana, cocoa powder and 2 teaspoons water to a food processor. Blitz until smooth. Pour into the bottom of the six ice lolly moulds. Lightly tap the moulds to remove any air bubbles. Pop into the freezer for 10 minutes.

While the chocolate layer is setting, make the white layer. Add the banana and 2 teaspoons water to the food processor and blitz until smooth. Once the chocolate layer has set a little, spoon the banana on top. Again, lightly tap the moulds to remove any air bubbles. Put back into the freezer for 10 minutes.

While the white layer sets, add the strawberries and banana to the food processor and blitz until smooth. Once the white layer has set a little, spoon the strawberry layer on top. Again, lightly tap the moulds to remove any air bubbles. Insert the lolly sticks and freeze overnight until the ice pops have set solid.

Add the chocolate to a small bowl and microwave in 30-second intervals until melted (or see Tip for doing this on the hob). Remove the ice pops from the moulds, spoon a little of the melted chocolate on top of each and sprinkle with the crushed Oreo biscuits.

TIP: If you don't have a microwave, melt the chocolate on the hob. Place the pieces in a heatproof bowl and set over a small pan of boiling water, making sure the bottom of the bowl does not touch the water. Stir the chocolate until melted.

APPLE FRITTERS

🕐 **10 MINS**   🍲 **VARIABLE** (SEE BELOW)   ✕ **SERVES 4**

PER SERVING:
(4 FRITTERS PER SERVING)
207 KCAL / 39G CARBS

SPECIAL EQUIPMENT
Stick blender or food processor

2 medium slices of white bread
1–2 tsp ground cinnamon, to taste
4 tbsp cornflour
1 medium egg, beaten
4 Granny Smith dessert apples, peeled, cored and cut into 1cm (½in)-thick rings (prepared weight 280g)
low-calorie cooking spray

TO ACCOMPANY *(optional)*
½ tbsp clear honey
   (+ 32 kcal per serving),
½ tbsp maple syrup
   (+ 26 kcal per serving)
or ½ tbsp golden syrup alternative fruit syrup (we like Sweet Freedom;
   + 19 kcal per serving)

We can't get enough of these crispy, cinnamon and breadcrumb-coated apple rings. Unlike high-calorie battered and deep-fried versions, our Apple Fritters are light, sweet and ready in a flash. We find it's best to use Granny Smith apples for this recipe, as they hold their shape nicely when you cook them. Whether you pop them in the oven or the air fryer, these little fritters make for a moreish snack at any time of day!

Weekly Indulgence ─────────────────

OVEN METHOD
🍲 **20 MINS**

Preheat the oven to 220°C (fan 200°C/gas mark 7) and line a baking tray with a sheet of non-stick baking paper.

Place the bread in a food processor or use a stick blender to blitz into fine breadcrumbs. Place the breadcrumbs on a medium plate and add the cinnamon. Mix thoroughly with clean fingertips.

Place the cornflour on a second medium plate and the beaten egg on a third medium plate. Place the plates in a row starting with the cornflour, then the egg and finally the cinnamon breadcrumbs. Dip the apple rings, one at a time, in the cornflour to lightly coat all over. Then dip into the beaten egg. Lastly, dip the apple rings in the cinnamon breadcrumbs to thoroughly coat. Repeat until all the apple rings are coated.

Place the apple rings on the lined baking tray in a single layer, leaving a space between each. Spray the tops of the fritters with low-calorie cooking spray and place in the oven to bake for 10 minutes.

Turn the apple fritters over and spray again with low-calorie cooking spray. Return to the oven and continue to bake for a further 10 minutes, until the apple is soft when tested with a small sharp knife, and the coating is golden brown and crisp.

Serve alone or with clear honey, maple syrup, golden syrup alternative fruit syrup or other accompaniment of your choice.

AIR-FRYER METHOD
🍲 14 MINS

SPECIAL EQUIPMENT
Air fryer

Place the bread in a food processor or use a stick blender to blitz into fine breadcrumbs. Place the breadcrumbs on a medium plate and add the cinnamon. Mix thoroughly with clean fingertips.

Place the cornflour on a second medium plate and the beaten egg on a third medium plate. Place the plates in a row starting with the cornflour, then the egg and finally the cinnamon breadcrumbs.

Dip the apple rings, one at a time, in the cornflour to lightly coat all over. Then dip into the beaten egg. Lastly, dip the apple rings in the cinnamon breadcrumbs to thoroughly coat. Repeat until all the apple rings are coated.

Meanwhile, preheat the air fryer to 190°C. Place the apple rings in the air-fryer basket, in a single layer, leaving space between each. You will probably need to cook the fritters in several batches depending on the capacity of your air fryer.

Spray with low-calorie cooking spray and cook for 7 minutes.

Turn the apple fritters over and spray again with low-calorie cooking spray. Continue to cook for a further 7 minutes, until the apple is soft when tested with a small sharp knife, and the coating is golden brown and crisp.

Serve alone or with clear honey, maple syrup, golden syrup alternative fruit syrup or other accompaniment of your choice.

TIPS: Make sure to cut the apples into 1cm (½in)-thick rings so that they cook in the time stated. If you haven't got a food processor or stick blender, you can use a grater to make the breadcrumbs.

VEGGIE

FREEZE ME

ORANGE RICOTTA CAKE

🕐 **15 MINS**   🗑 **30 MINS**   ✕ **SERVES 16**

PER SERVING:
138 KCAL / 15G CARBS

SPECIAL EQUIPMENT
20cm (8in) square cake tin
Electric whisk

low-calorie cooking spray
100g reduced-fat butter
250g ricotta
120g white granulated
  sweetener, plus 2 tbsp
3 medium eggs
grated zest and juice of
  1 orange
100g self-raising flour
50g ground almonds

Our Orange Ricotta Cake falls somewhere between an Italian lemon ricotta cake and a lemon drizzle cake. You'd be forgiven for expecting a light, fluffy-in-the-middle cake; instead, the silky ricotta and almonds make for a gloriously dense, creamy-textured sponge. It's a delight while chilled, but we can't deny that a whole new level of velvety luxury is unlocked when this orange-infused pud is warmed through.

Everyday Light ———————————————

Preheat the oven to 180°C (fan 160°C/gas mark 4). Spray the cake tin with low-calorie cooking spray and line with non-stick baking paper.

Allow the butter and ricotta to come to room temperature. Place in a mixing bowl with the 120g granulated sweetener and beat using an electric whisk until pale and fluffy. Beat in the eggs one at a time.

Add the orange zest, flour and ground almonds and whisk on low until well combined. It will only take a few seconds. Don't over-whisk at this stage as overworking the flour can make the cake tough or rubbery!

Pour into the prepared tin and place in the centre of the oven.

Bake for 30 minutes. This cake doesn't brown as much as a sponge cake, but you will be able to tell when it is cooked as it will be springy and a skewer inserted into the middle will come out clean.

Mix together the orange juice and the 2 tablespoons of granulated sweetener and pour over the top of the cake while it is still hot.

Leave to cool before turning out and cutting into sixteen pieces. The cake may 'deflate' a little when removed from the oven. This is perfectly normal.

TIPS: You can replace the sweetener with the same amount of sugar, if you prefer. This will increase the calories. We used reduced-fat butter in this recipe but reduced-fat spread will work fine too!

VEGGIE

GLUTEN FREE

USE GF PASTRY

CREAMY RASPBERRY SLICES

🕐 **25 MINS**   🍲 **10 MINS**   ✕ **MAKES 6**

PER SERVING:
313 KCAL / 37G CARBS

SPECIAL EQUIPMENT
Piping bag with 1cm (½in) round nozzle

375g ready-rolled light puff pastry sheet, about 30 x 26cm (12 x 10in)

½ medium egg, beaten with a fork

150g reduced-fat cream cheese

50g fat-free Greek-style yoghurt

a few drops of vanilla extract, or to taste

15g white granulated sweetener

200g fresh raspberries

½ tsp icing sugar

A cream slice is one of those things that feels like it should be off the menu when you're watching what you eat. Too delicious to miss out on, we've created a slimming-friendly version, and it's every bit as decadent as you'd expect. Our light puff pastry slices are sandwiched together with an unmissable layer of sweetened cream cheese mixed with fat-free Greek yoghurt. We've even nestled some beautiful fresh raspberries right in the middle, to make a teatime treat that you'll look forward to all day.

Special Occasion ─────────

Preheat the oven to 220°C (fan 200°C/gas mark 7).

Line two baking trays with non-stick baking paper. Unroll the pastry, leaving it on the paper packaging, and cut into twelve 5 x 13cm (2 x 5in) rectangles. Carefully remove from their packing paper and place six on each lined baking tray, making sure they are well spaced out.

Prick the tops all over with a fork and brush with beaten egg.

Place both trays in the oven for 8–10 minutes, until the pastry has risen a little and is golden brown. You may need to swap the trays around halfway through to ensure even cooking.

Remove from the oven, transfer to a cooling rack and leave to cool completely.

To make the creamy filling, mix together the cream cheese, yoghurt, vanilla extract and sweetener in a medium bowl until smooth.

Turn the pastry slices over. Divide the creamy filling between six of the pastry slices – simply spread it out evenly with a knife, or for more of a patisserie look, fill the piping bag and pipe little dots all over the surface.

Divide the raspberries between six of the pastry slices, placing them upright in a single layer.

Place the remaining pastry slices on top of the raspberries. Dust lightly with the icing sugar and serve.

TIP: If you prefer, you can make these Creamy Raspberry Slices half the size to reduce the calories per serving by half.

LEMON CURD SWISS ROLL

🕐 **25 MINS**   🍲 **15 MINS**   ✕ **SERVES 10**

PER SERVING:
126 KCAL /23G CARBS

SPECIAL EQUIPMENT
32.5 x 22.5cm (13 x 9in)
 Swiss roll tin
Electric whisk

low-calorie cooking spray
4 medium eggs
50g white granulated
 sweetener
50g caster sugar
finely grated zest of
 1 medium lemon
100g self-raising flour
90g lemon curd

TO DECORATE
¼ tsp icing sugar, for
 dusting
10 lemon slices (optional)
10 small mint sprigs
 (optional)

TIPS: Make sure to use an electric whisk to whisk the sponge mixture to a thick, pale and creamy consistency. It will be very difficult to do this by hand. It is also important to roll the sponge while it's still warm otherwise it won't roll up properly.

Our slimming-friendly version of a Swiss roll is guaranteed to put a smile on anyone's face. Light airy sponge was made to go with zingy sweet lemon curd, and you won't regret giving this recipe a try. Rolled up and cut into swirled slices, our citrusy treat is finished with a simple dusting of icing sugar (you can add a sprig of mint and a few lemon slices if you're feeling fancy!). Put the kettle on and get comfy – you'll want to sit back and enjoy every bite.

Everyday Light ─────────────────────

Preheat the oven to 180°C (fan 160°C/gas mark 4). Grease the Swiss roll tin with low-calorie cooking spray and line the base and sides with a sheet of non-stick baking paper.

Place the eggs, granulated sweetener and caster sugar in a large bowl. Use an electric whisk to whisk on high speed for 10 minutes until very thick, pale and creamy. The mixture should hold a 'ribbon' trail when the whisk heads are lifted out.

Add the lemon zest. Sift the flour into the mixture a little at a time and use a large spoon to gently fold in until just combined. Take care not to over-mix as you don't want to knock out the air you have incorporated.

Scrape into the prepared tin and gently spread out evenly.

Bake in the preheated oven for 10–15 minutes, until golden. Gently press the centre of the sponge, it should spring back when it's ready and leave no indent.

Turn the cooked sponge out of the tin onto a sheet of non-stick baking paper, top side down. Carefully peel off the lining paper and discard. Trim off the crusty edges from the two long sides. Using a round-bladed knife, score a line along the narrow end nearest to you, about 2.5cm (1in) in from the edge.

While the sponge is still warm, and starting with the scored narrow end, carefully roll up into a Swiss roll, using the non-stick baking paper to help you. Place seam side down and leave to cool completely on the paper sheet.

Gently unroll the cooled sponge out on the paper sheet and spread the lemon curd evenly over the surface. Roll up to form a Swiss roll, finishing seam side down.

Dust with a little icing sugar and use a large serrated knife to cut into ten slices. Place each slice on a small plate and decorate, if you wish, with a slice of lemon and a small sprig of mint.

VEGGIE

 FREEZE ME

 SUPER SAVER · SUPER SAVER ·

APPLE CRUMBLE SQUARES

🕐 **15 MINS**　🍲 **45–50 MINS**　✕ **MAKES 16**

PER SQUARE:
78 KCAL / 18G CARBS

SPECIAL EQUIPMENT
20cm (8in) square baking tin

2 cooking apples,
　about 250g
40g white granulated
　sweetener
1 tbsp lemon juice
1 tbsp cornflour

FOR THE CRUMBLE
300g self-raising flour
60g white granulated
　sweetener
60g reduced-fat spread
1 medium egg
1 tbsp skimmed milk
1 tsp vanilla extract

In need of a mid-afternoon pick-me-up? Let the cosy, comforting flavours of these Apple Crumble Squares work their magic. You'll find a layer of sweetened apple pieces baked into the centre of our golden brown crumble mixture. You don't even need to stew down your apples before baking – everything cooks together in one tin (hurray for less washing up!). It's impossible to find anything easier or more delicious to enjoy with a cuppa!

Everyday Light ─────────────────────

Preheat the oven to 200°C (fan 180°C/gas mark 6) and line the tin with non-stick baking paper.

First, make the crumble. In a mixing bowl, add the flour and sweetener and stir to combine. Rub the reduced-fat spread into the flour mixture until it forms a breadcrumb texture.

Add the egg, milk and vanilla to a small bowl and whisk with a fork until combined. Pour into the flour mixture and use your hands to combine until just starting to stick together in a larger breadcrumb texture.

Peel the apples and remove the cores. Dice the apples and add to a bowl with the sweetener, lemon juice and cornflour. Toss to coat.

Add half the crumble mixture to the tin and firmly press flat with your fingers to cover the bottom of the tin.

Scatter the apple over the crumble base in an even layer. Scatter the remaining crumble mixture over the top of the fruit and press with your fingers to encase the apple between the two layers.

Bake in the oven for 45–50 minutes, until the top is golden brown and the apple is soft when a knife is inserted.

Remove from the oven and leave to cool completely in the tin. Cut into sixteen squares and serve.

VEGGIE

FREEZE ME

WITHOUT THE
CREAM AND
CHOCOLATE
POWDER

SUPER SAVER · SUPER SAVER ·

CAPPUCCINO LAVA CAKES

🕐 **10 MINS**   📷 **VARIABLE** (SEE BELOW)   ✕ **MAKES 4**

PER SERVING:
159 KCAL /19G CARBS

SPECIAL EQUIPMENT
4 x 125ml ovenproof ramekin dishes
Electric whisk

45g reduced-fat spread, plus
  a little extra for greasing
45g self-raising flour
1 tsp baking powder
25g white granulated
  sweetener
1 tbsp medium-strength
  instant coffee powder
2 medium eggs
1 tsp vanilla extract
4 squares of milk chocolate

FOR THE TOP
reduced-fat aerosol cream,
  to swirl on top
½ tsp drinking chocolate
  powder, for dusting

We can't think of a better excuse to crack out our ramekins than these Cappuccino Lava Cakes. Ready to pop in the oven (or microwave!) after just 10 minutes of preparation, they're an easy, sweet pick-me-up. Inspired by frothy cappuccino indulgence, we've topped each lava cake with a swirl of reduced-fat aerosol cream and a dusting of chocolate powder. If that doesn't win your heart, there's no doubt the oozy, melted milk chocolate centre will.

Everyday Light ─────────────────────

OVEN METHOD
📷 **10 MINS**

Preheat the oven to 180°C (fan 160°C/gas mark 4). Grease the ramekin dishes with a little of the reduced-fat spread.

Place the self-raising flour, baking powder, sweetener, coffee powder, reduced-fat spread, eggs and vanilla extract in a medium mixing bowl. Beat together for 1–2 minutes using an electric whisk or wooden spoon until smooth and creamy.

Divide the mixture evenly between the ramekin dishes. Place a chocolate square in the centre of each.

Put on a baking tray and bake in the oven for 8–10 minutes, until risen and spongy but still runny in the centre.

Remove from the oven and leave to stand for 5 minutes. Pipe a swirl of aerosol cream on top of each cake and dust with a little chocolate powder. Serve at once.

TIP: Take care not to overcook otherwise you won't get a melting chocolate centre. Follow the timings carefully and remove from the oven or microwave while still runny in the centre. Leave to stand for 5 minutes and then you should have the perfect melting centre.

MICROWAVE METHOD
🍲 1½–2 MINS

Grease the ramekin dishes with a little of the reduced
-fat spread.

Place the self-raising flour, baking powder, sweetener,
coffee powder, reduced-fat spread, eggs and vanilla
extract in a medium mixing bowl. Beat together for
1–2 minutes using an electric whisk or wooden spoon until
smooth and creamy.

Divide the mixture evenly between the ramekin dishes.

Place a chocolate square in the centre of each.

Place all four ramekins on the microwave turntable,
evenly spaced apart. Cover loosely with cling film and
cook on high for 1½–2 minutes. Check on the cakes after
about a minute and continue cooking if needed. The
cakes will be ready when they're risen and spongy but
still runny in the centre. Leave to stand for 5 minutes,
then remove the cling film.

Pipe a swirl of aerosol cream on top of each cake and
dust with a little chocolate powder. Serve at once.

TIPS: If you only have instant coffee granules rather than
powder, you can place them in a sealed food bag and use
something heavy such as a rolling pin to crush them into a
fine powder. To freeze the cooled cakes, firstly make sure your
ramekins are freezerproof. Then wrap them in cling film or foil
and pack in a freezerproof container and freeze. Defrost in
the fridge, then cover loosely with cling film and reheat in the
microwave for about 30 seconds.

NORWEGIAN-STYLE APPLE CAKE

VEGGIE

FREEZE ME

🕐 **20 MINS**   🪣 **55 MINS**   ✕ **SERVES 16**

PER SERVING:
88 KCAL /16G CARBS

SPECIAL EQUIPMENT
20cm (8in) square cake tin
Electric whisk

3 small eating apples (any kind), peeled, cored and thinly sliced (prepared weight 270g)
2 tsp lemon juice
120g reduced-fat spread, plus a little extra for greasing
60g white granulated sweetener
60g caster sugar
120g self-raising flour
2 medium eggs
1 tsp baking powder
1¼ tsp ground cinnamon

Warm up with our cosy Norwegian-style Apple Cake! Lightly spiced and oh-so-moist, this fruity cake pairs the sweetness of baked apples with a sprinkle of cinnamon. We can't get enough of the pudding-y texture of this easy-to-make baked treat. Delicious on its own, you could take it up a notch with a glug of low-calorie custard too. Save a slice for the ultimate mid-afternoon tea break snack!

Everyday Light

Preheat the oven to 180°C (fan 160°C/gas mark 4). Grease and line the base and sides of the tin with non-stick baking paper.

Place the apple slices in a small bowl and sprinkle the lemon juice over. Toss to completely coat. This will stop the apples from discolouring.

Place the reduced-fat spread, granulated sweetener, caster sugar, self-raising flour, eggs, baking powder and 1 teaspoon of the ground cinnamon in a medium bowl. Mix with an electric whisk or wooden spoon for 1–2 minutes, until smooth.

Place half of the cake mixture in the prepared tin and spread out.

Place half of the apple slices on top of the cake mixture, in a single layer. There's no need to arrange these apple slices as they will be hidden inside the cake.

Place the remaining cake mixture on top of the apples and spread it out. Place the remaining apple slices on top in a single layer. You can arrange them in rows or go for a more casual, rustic arrangement.

Sprinkle the top with the remaining cinnamon and bake in the preheated oven for 50–55 minutes. The cake should be golden brown on top and a knife inserted into the centre should come out clean. Remove from the oven and leave in the tin for 10 minutes.

Use the lining paper to carefully lift the cake out of the tin and place on a work surface, then cut the cake into sixteen squares using a large serrated knife. Serve warm or cold.

TIP: Slice the apples thinly so that they cook through in the stated time.

USE VEGAN
PASTRY

STRAWBERRY GALETTE

🕐 **5 MINS**   🍲 **25 MINS**   ✕ **SERVES 4**

PER SERVING:
326 KCAL /29G CARBS

20cm (8in) circle of ready-
  rolled puff pastry, about
  300g
300g strawberries, stalks
  removed and fruit sliced
1 tsp white granulated
  sweetener

Proof that the tastiest sweet treats don't have to be
complicated, you won't believe how short the ingredients
list is for our Strawberry Galette. Once the strawberry
slices are tucked in nicely at the centre of your puff pastry
base, pop it in the oven and bake to golden perfection.
We can't get enough of the syrupy centre of warmed-
up strawberries! Plus, this rustic, pie-like dish never has
to be the same twice – try a different combination of
strawberries, raspberries or blueberries each time and
keep your fruity filling fresh.

Special Occasion

Preheat the oven to 210°C (fan 190°C/gas mark 6) and line
a baking tray with greaseproof paper.

Place the circle of puff pastry onto the lined tray.

Add the strawberries to the centre of the puff pastry and
loosely fold over the edges to create a border.

Using a pastry brush, brush the exposed pastry edge with
2 teaspoons of cold water. Sprinkle the sweetener over the
strawberries and pastry edge.

Pop into the oven and bake for 25 minutes until the pastry
crust is golden brown, and the strawberries are softened
and syrupy. Serve.

LEMON MERINGUE POTS

🕐 **20 MINS** 🍲 **20 MINS** ✕ **SERVES 4**

PER SERVING:
268 KCAL / 48G CARBS

SPECIAL EQUIPMENT
Food processor or mini chopper
  (optional)
4 x 125ml ovenproof
  ramekin dishes
Electric whisk

4 reduced-fat digestive
  biscuits
20g reduced-fat spread

FOR THE LEMON FILLING
finely grated zest and juice
  of 2 medium lemons (60ml)
3 tbsp white granulated
  sweetener
3 tbsp cornflour
2 medium egg yolks, broken
  up with a fork

FOR THE MERINGUES
2 medium egg whites
2 tbsp white granulated
  sweetener
2 tbsp caster sugar

If citrusy puddings are your go-to, you need to try these Lemon Meringue Pots. Brimming with bold, zesty flavours, we've topped each delightful little pot with light, fluffy meringue swirls. Layered on top of a reduced-fat digestive biscuit base, the oh-so-indulgent sweetened lemon centre tastes far higher in calories than it actually is. Inspired by lemon meringue pie, our golden-topped pots are so good that you'll never miss the pastry!

Weekly Indulgence ———————————————

Preheat the oven to 180°C (fan 160°C/gas mark 4). Place the biscuits in a food processor or mini chopper and blitz until they resemble fine breadcrumbs. If you don't have a food processor or mini chopper, place the biscuits in a food bag, seal and crush with a rolling pin.

Place the reduced-fat spread in a small bowl and microwave for 30 seconds–1 minute, or until just melted. If you don't have a microwave, do this in a small pan over a low heat. Stir in the biscuit crumbs until all the crumbs are coated.

Divide the biscuit mixture between the ovenproof ramekin dishes. Press down with the back of a teaspoon to make an even layer in each dish. Place in the fridge.

Meanwhile, make the lemon filling. Place the lemon juice in a small saucepan with 240ml cold water. Add the lemon zest and white granulated sweetener.

Mix the cornflour with 3 tablespoons of cold water and stir until smooth. Stir into the lemon mixture in the small saucepan.

Place over a medium heat and bring to the boil, stirring constantly with a wooden spoon or balloon whisk. As soon as the mixture is boiling, reduce the heat and simmer gently for 4–5 minutes, stirring constantly, until thickened and glossy. Remove from the heat and leave to cool for a few minutes.

After cooling for a few minutes off the heat, stir in the egg yolks, a little at a time. Stir well between each addition with a wooden spoon or balloon whisk until smooth. Make sure to do this off the heat, otherwise you may get bits of cooked egg in your filling. If this happens, just strain it through a sieve to remove any bits.

Remove the ramekin dishes from the fridge. Divide the lemon mixture evenly between the four ramekin dishes, pouring on top of the biscuit layer.

To make the meringue mixture, place the egg whites in a large, clean bowl. Beat using an electric whisk for 1–2 minutes on high speed, until stiff peaks are formed. Whisk in the granulated sweetener and caster sugar a little at a time, then whisk for a further minute on high speed. You should have a stiff, glossy meringue.

Place the ramekin dishes on a baking tray. Divide the meringue between the ramekins, spreading over the lemon layer, right to the edge of the dishes to seal. Swirl the meringue into peaks. Place in the oven and bake for 8–10 minutes until golden. Serve at once.

.

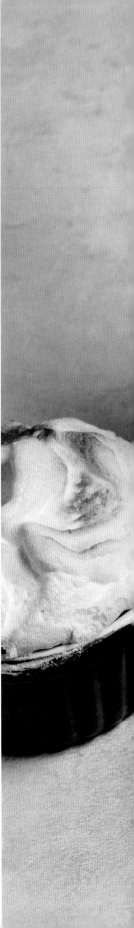

TIPS: When making the meringue, ensure the bowl and whisk heads are very clean and free from grease otherwise the egg whites won't whisk properly. Place the meringue on top of the lemon layer whilst it's still a little warm. This will help the meringue to seal onto the lemon layer and not slide off. Don't leave your Lemon Meringue Pots in the oven longer than 10 minutes, as the lemon layer may become runny.

VEGGIE

FREEZE ME

LOW CARB

SUPER SAVER · SUPER SAVER ·

RASPBERRY COOKIE BROWNIES

🕐 **5 MINS**   🍲 **8–10 MINS**   ✗ **SERVES 12**

PER BROWNIE:
129 KCAL /14G CARBS

SPECIAL EQUIPMENT
12-hole silicone muffin tin

low-calorie cooking spray
100g self-raising flour
50g reduced-fat spread
4 tbsp white granulated
　sweetener
4 medium eggs
3 tbsp cocoa powder
1 tsp baking powder
6 raspberries, sliced in half
20g bag of mini chocolate
　sandwich biscuits,
　quartered
20g milk chocolate, finely
　chopped

You'd never guess these loaded brownies are less than 130 calories each! We all need a chocolate fix from time to time, and this slimming-friendly recipe never disappoints. As if squidgy chocolate brownie isn't enough, we've sprinkled milk chocolate chunks, crumbled biscuits and raspberry pieces on top before baking them to perfection. Psst . . . you want to take these out of the oven while they're ever so slightly undercooked and let them cool briefly in the tin!

Everyday Light —————————————————————

Preheat the oven to 190°C (fan 170°C/gas mark 5). Spray the twelve holes of the silicone muffin tin with a little low-calorie cooking spray.

Place the self-raising flour, reduced-fat spread, granulated sweetener, eggs, cocoa powder and baking powder into a large mixing bowl and mix thoroughly. It's best to use a wooden spoon to prevent over-mixing.

Pour the mixture into the silicone muffin tin, dividing it evenly between the twelve holes. Add half a raspberry to the top of each brownie. Sprinkle over the biscuit and chocolate pieces. Place in the oven and bake for 8–10 minutes until slightly risen and set.

Leave to cool in the tin for a few minutes and then transfer to a cooling rack. Serve.

EVE'S PUDDING

🕐 **15 MINS**   🍲 **50 MINS**   🍴 **SERVES 6**

PER SERVING:
271 KCAL / 50G CARBS

SPECIAL EQUIPMENT
18 x 27cm (7 x 10½in)
   ovenproof dish
Electric whisk (optional)

600g Bramley cooking
   apples, peeled, cored and
   thinly sliced
2 tbsp white granulated
   sweetener
finely grated zest and juice
   of 1 lemon
20g raisins
½ tsp ground cinnamon
½ tsp icing sugar, for dusting

FOR THE SPONGE TOPPING
120g reduced-fat spread, plus
   a little extra for greasing
120g self-raising flour
60g white granulated
   sweetener
60g caster sugar
1 tsp baking powder
2 medium eggs

Our take on a classic British bake, the flavours in this slimming-friendly Eve's Pudding are sure to warm you right up. Using a simple list of easy lower-calorie ingredients, we've recreated all the hearty comfort of traditional versions without breaking the bank. The layer of juicy, cinnamon-infused apples is the real treat at the bottom of every bowlful. Once the sponge is golden brown, that's your cue to pop the kettle on. Finish the top with a dusting of icing sugar and enjoy your new favourite cuppa companion!

Weekly Indulgence

Preheat the oven to 180°C (fan 160°C/gas mark 4) and grease the ovenproof dish with a little reduced-fat spread.

In a medium bowl, mix the apples, the 2 tablespoons of granulated sweetener, lemon zest, lemon juice, raisins and ground cinnamon until combined.

Put the apple mixture into the greased dish and spread out evenly.

To make the sponge topping, place the flour, reduced-fat spread, granulated sweetener, caster sugar, baking powder and eggs into a medium mixing bowl. Beat for 1–2 minutes with an electric whisk or wooden spoon until smooth.

Scrape the sponge mixture out of the bowl onto the apples in the ovenproof dish. Spread out evenly, making sure that the apples are completely covered.

Place the dish on a baking tray and place in the oven. Bake for 45–50 minutes, until the apples are just tender when pierced with a sharp knife and the sponge is golden brown.

Remove from the oven, dust the top with the icing sugar, and serve.

TIP: Make sure to slice the apples evenly and very thinly so that they cook properly.

USE GF FLOUR
AND BAKING
POWDER

HOT CHOCOLATE MICROWAVE MUG CAKES

🕐 **5 MINS**   🍲 **90 SECS**   ✕ **MAKES 2**

PER SERVING:
193 KCAL / 29G CARBS

SPECIAL EQUIPMENT
2 x 200ml microwave-safe mugs or cups
Electric whisk (optional)

20g reduced-fat spread, softened, plus a little extra for greasing
20g self-raising flour
½ tsp baking powder
10g caster sugar
10g white granulated sweetener
1 medium egg
2 tbsp low-calorie chocolate syrup (we used Choc Shot made by Sweet Freedom)

FOR THE TOP
reduced-fat aerosol cream, to swirl on top
10 pink and white mini marshmallows (2g)
1 tsp low-calorie chocolate syrup, to drizzle on top

A mug cake is always a good idea! We've taken all the best bits of an indulgent, whipped cream-topped hot chocolate and turned it into a slimming-friendly pud you can make in next to no time. Each perfectly portioned chocolate cake is served with a swirl of reduced-fat aerosol cream, a sprinkle of mini marshmallows and a drizzle of low-calorie chocolate sauce. There's no reason to skip dessert when it's this quick, easy and delicious!

Everyday Light

Grease the microwave-safe mugs or cups with a little extra reduced-fat spread.

Place the flour, baking powder, caster sugar, granulated sweetener, reduced-fat spread, egg and chocolate syrup in a small mixing bowl. Beat with an electric whisk or wooden spoon for 1 minute until smooth.

Scrape the cake mixture from the bowl and into the greased mugs or cups using a rubber spatula. Cover loosely with cling film, leaving a small vent at one edge. Place both mugs on the microwave turntable and microwave on high for 90 seconds (see Tip about different microwaves below). The cakes will rise above the rim of the mug during cooking, so make sure the covering is loose enough to allow them to rise. After cooking, the cakes will drop down to be about level with the rim of the mugs. They will be ready when a small sharp knife is inserted and it comes out clean.

Remove the cooked cakes from the microwave and remove the coverings. Leave to stand for 5 minutes.

After standing for 5 minutes, pipe a swirl of aerosol cream on top of each cake. Scatter five marshmallows on top. Drizzle with ½ teaspoon of low-calorie chocolate syrup and serve at once.

TIP: We used an 800-watt microwave oven, but the mug cakes may take a little more or less cooking time depending on the power of your microwave.

LEMON DRIZZLE SWIRLS

🕐 **10 MINS**   🍲 **20 MINS**   ✕ **MAKES 16**

PER SWIRL:
100 KCAL / 13G CARBS

2 tbsp lemon curd
2 tsp lemon juice
1 tsp finely grated lemon zest
320g ready-rolled light puff
  pastry sheet

FOR THE DRIZZLE
1 tbsp reduced-fat cream
  cheese
1 tsp lemon juice
1 tsp icing sugar

Inspired by two much-loved desserts, these light pastry treats are what you get when you cross a cinnamon roll with lemon drizzle cake. Using only a handful of ingredients, it takes just half an hour to bake a batch to enjoy with your next cuppa. We've cut down on calories by using reduced-fat cream cheese to make the citrusy, lemon-infused drizzle for the topping. Sweet, zesty and so moreish, you'll be pleased to know these are just 100 calories each!

Everyday Light ——————————————

Preheat the oven to 190°C (fan 170°C/gas mark 5) and line a baking tray with non-stick baking paper.

In a bowl, combine the lemon curd, lemon juice and lemon zest and mix until smooth. Unroll the pastry sheet, leaving it on the paper packaging, and place on your work surface.

Spread the lemon curd mixture over the pastry, leaving a 1cm (½in) gap along the long edges. Roll up the pastry, starting with the long edge, using the paper packaging to help you.

Keep rolling until you have made a 'Swiss roll'. When you have finished rolling up the pastry, make sure it is seam side down.

Use a large serrated knife, such as a bread knife, to carefully cut into sixteen spiral-shaped slices. Place the swirls flat side down onto the lined baking tray, leaving gaps between each swirl.

Place the tray in the oven and bake for 20 minutes, until golden and crisp. Transfer the swirls to a cooling rack to cool completely.

While the swirls are cooling, combine the cream cheese, lemon juice and icing sugar and mix until smooth. Once cool, drizzle over the cream cheese mixture and serve.

MALT CHOCOLATE ICE CREAM

🕐 **10 MINS***   🗑 **NO-COOK**   ✕ **SERVES 4**

*PLUS OVERNIGHT AND 4 HRS FREEZING

PER SERVING:
235 KCAL / 42G CARBS

SPECIAL EQUIPMENT
Food processor
1-litre freezer-proof container

4 ripe medium bananas,
   about 100g each, peeled
   and sliced
3 tbsp Ovaltine Original Light
   malted instant drink powder
4 tsp low-calorie chocolate
   syrup
37g bag Maltesers, lightly
   crushed
4 malted milk biscuits, lightly
   crushed

TO SERVE
4 x waffle ice cream cones
   (+ 49 kcal per serving)

Swirled with crushed Maltesers, crumbled biscuits and chocolate syrup, you'd never think a scoop of this loaded ice cream could be slimming friendly (or so easy to make!). Give your overripe bananas a new lease of life by blending them with malty and chocolatey ingredients, until you have a creamy frozen treat that's perfect for sunny days and cosy nights alike. Grab a spoon . . . you won't be able to resist this one!

Weekly Indulgence ———————————

Place the sliced bananas in a single layer on a baking tray and pop in the freezer overnight.

Lift the frozen banana slices out of the freezer 5 minutes before you are ready to make the ice cream, so that they can soften slightly.

Add the frozen sliced banana to the food processor and blitz until thick and smooth. You may find adding a splash of water helps if the banana is too stiff.

Scrape the blitzed banana into a mixing bowl and add the Ovaltine powder and 3 teaspoons of the low-calorie chocolate syrup. Stir until combined.

Add half of the crushed biscuits and half of the crushed Maltesers and fold in until they have swirled through the banana mixture to give a marbled effect.

Transfer to a 1-litre freezer-proof container, spread out and sprinkle with the remaining crushed biscuits and Maltesers. Drizzle over the remaining low-calorie chocolate syrup.

Cover with a lid or cling film and pop back into the freezer for 4 hours to firm up.

When ready to serve, remove from the freezer and leave to soften for about 10 minutes before serving up in waffle cones.

TIP: This is a great recipe for using up overripe bananas. They are perfect when the skins are very spotted as this will ensure that they are nice and sweet.

VEGGIE

 GLUTEN FREE

 LOW CARB

PEANUT BUTTER *and* CHOCOLATE MOUSSE

 SUPER SAVER · SUPER SAVER

🕐 **10 MINS***   🍲 **30 SECS**   ✕ **SERVES 4**

***PLUS 30 MINS CHILLING**

PER SERVING:
230 KCAL / 8.8G CARBS

SPECIAL EQUIPMENT
Electric whisk
4 x 125ml ramekin dishes

100ml light double cream
  alternative
40g smooth peanut butter
40g chocolate spread
100g fat-free Greek-style
  yoghurt
½ tsp vanilla extract
4g roasted salted peanuts,
  roughly crushed

You'll want to save a little bit of room after your dinner for this decadent-tasting dessert. Our Peanut Butter and Chocolate Mousse draws on a winning flavour combination. This recipe is super simple, but so satisfying, with a silky, airy mousse that's made by whipping up a light double cream alternative. Swirl the two flavours together just enough to give a lovely marbled effect, then top with a sprinkle of crushed roasted salted peanuts.

Weekly Indulgence

Place the light double cream alternative in a medium mixing bowl. Whisk with an electric whisk, on high speed, for about 2 minutes until soft peaks are formed. Take care not to over-whisk the cream alternative otherwise it will become too stiff to fold in the remaining ingredients.

Place the peanut butter in a small microwavable bowl or cup, and the chocolate spread in another small microwavable bowl or cup. Microwave until completely smooth and runny. You can do this by placing both bowls in the microwave together and heating in small bursts until melted and completely smooth and runny. Alternatively, place the small bowls or cups in a larger bowl containing boiling water and stir for about 2 minutes.

Add the yoghurt and vanilla extract to the bowl with the whipped cream alternative. Fold in gently using a rubber spatula or large metal spoon until completely combined. Take care not to knock the air out of the mixture.

Divide the mixture in half, placing half in another medium bowl.

Add the melted peanut butter to one bowl and fold in gently using a rubber spatula or large metal spoon until completely combined. Add the melted chocolate spread to the other bowl and fold in gently until completely combined.

Divide the peanut butter mousse between the four ramekin dishes, placing it on one side of the dishes. Divide the chocolate mousse between the dishes, placing it on the other side of the dishes.

Use a teaspoon to swirl the peanut butter mousse with the chocolate mousse a little. Take care not to over-mix; you still need to see the two different flavours.

Sprinkle the tops with the crushed peanuts, place in the fridge to chill for about 30 minutes and serve.

VEGGIE

DAIRY FREE

USE DF MILK
AND YOGHURT

SUPER SAVER · SUPER SAVER ·

PINEAPPLE FRITTERS

🕐 8 MINS 🍲 8 MINS ✕ SERVES 4

PER SERVING:
246 KCAL / 43G CARBS

100g self-raising flour
100ml skimmed milk
1 medium egg, beaten
pinch of salt
low-calorie cooking spray
¼ tsp ground ginger
¼ tsp ground cinnamon
1 tsp white granulated
  sweetener
4 rings of fresh pineapple,
  about 175g each
2 tsp honey
4 tbsp fat-free Greek-style
  yoghurt

These zingy Pineapple Fritters are so good, you'll never be able to tell they're not deep-fried. We've saved on calories by frying our batter-covered pineapple rings with a spritz of low-calorie cooking spray. Once they're golden and crispy, we've coated them in a moreish dusting of ginger, cinnamon and sweetener. An easy sweet bite you can prepare in under 20 minutes, they're best enjoyed with a refreshing spoonful of our honey yoghurt – they go together like a dream!

Weekly Indulgence ————————————————

Place the flour, milk, egg and salt in a mixing bowl and whisk until smooth with a balloon whisk to make a batter.

Spray a frying pan with low-calorie cooking spray and set on a low-medium heat. Add the ginger, cinnamon and sweetener to a baking tray (give the tray a shake to distribute).

Take a pineapple ring and submerge it into the batter, flipping it over to coat on all sides. Allow any excess to drip off and place into the hot frying pan.

Cook the fritters one at a time for 1 minute and flip over; the batter should be golden brown and crispy around the edges. Cook the other side for another minute.

Once the first pineapple ring is cooked, place it onto the baking tray and then flip over to give a light coating of the cinnamon and ginger mix. Cook the rest of the pineapple rings.

Mix the honey with the yoghurt. Serve the pineapple fritters with a spoonful of the yoghurt.

TIPS: We found it best to cook one fritter at a time so as not to overcrowd the pan. You could also choose to drizzle the honey over the fritters and serve the yoghurt alongside.

SPRINKLE SPONGE

🕐 **10 MINS**   🗑 **25 MINS**   ✕ **SERVES 16**

USE GF FLOUR
AND BAKING
POWDER

PER SERVING:
71 KCAL /12G CARBS

SPECIAL EQUIPMENT
**20 x 22cm (8 x 8½in)
ovenproof dish
Electric whisk**

100g reduced-fat spread,
   plus a little extra for
   greasing
100g self-raising flour
50g white granulated
   sweetener
50g caster sugar
½ tsp baking powder
2 medium eggs
1 tsp vanilla extract

FOR THE TOPPING
2 tbsp icing sugar
1 tsp hundreds and
   thousands

Who remembers this sprinkled-topped cake from your school dinners? We've gone back to our childhood for the inspiration for this Sprinkle Sponge. Nostalgic and delicious in equal measure, our lighter recipe replaces half of the sugar with sweetener to keep the calories down. Rather than smothering the whole cake in icing, a small drizzle goes a long way; and you can't forget that all-important sprinkling of hundreds and thousands on the top.

Everyday Light ─────────────────────────

Preheat the oven to 180°C (fan 160°C/gas mark 4) and grease the ovenproof dish well with a little reduced-fat spread.

Put the flour, reduced-fat spread, granulated sweetener, caster sugar, baking powder, eggs and vanilla extract in a medium mixing bowl and beat together for 1–2 minutes with an electric whisk. Alternatively, you can use a wooden spoon, but it will take more effort.

Use a rubber spatula to scrape the mixture from the mixing bowl into the greased ovenproof dish and level the surface with a knife. Bake in the oven for 20–25 minutes, until risen and golden all over. To test if it's ready, insert a small sharp knife into the centre of the sponge: when the sponge is cooked the knife will come out clean. Leave the sponge in the ovenproof dish to cool.

Sift the icing sugar into a small bowl and stir in 1 teaspoon of cold water until smooth. Drizzle the icing over the cooled sponge and sprinkle over the hundreds and thousands.

Let the icing set, then cut into sixteen squares and serve!

WHITE CHOCOLATE *and* ORANGE CRÈME BRÛLÉE

🕐 **10 MINS**   🗑 **35 MINS**   ✕ **SERVES 6**

PER SERVING:
186 KCAL / 22G CARBS

SPECIAL EQUIPMENT
6 x 120ml ovenproof ramekins
Kitchen blowtorch (optional)

90g white chocolate, broken
  into squares
400ml skimmed milk
2 tbsp white granulated
  sweetener
1 tsp vanilla extract
grated zest of 1 orange
2 medium eggs
2 medium egg yolks
6 tsp caster sugar

You know you want to crack open the sweet topping on our luxurious White Chocolate and Orange Crème Brûlée! Every bit as crunchy on the outside and creamy in the middle as restaurant versions, we've brought together a cheap and cheerful combination of ingredients that'll make sure they're slimming-friendly too. Ideal for impressing your friends, each ramekin is filled with a zesty, orange-infused white chocolate cream you'll be dying to get your spoon into.

Everyday Light

Preheat the oven to 200°C (fan 180°C/gas mark 6).

Add the chocolate, milk, sweetener, vanilla extract and orange zest into a medium pan over a low heat. Allow the chocolate to melt, stirring continuously as the milk heats. When the milk is warm and the chocolate is completely melted, remove from the heat and allow to cool slightly.

In a mixing bowl, stir together the eggs and egg yolks. Gradually pour the infused milk and chocolate mixture into the mixing bowl, whisking continuously until completely combined.

Place the six ramekins into a deep ovenproof baking dish. Fill each ramekin with the mixture.

Fill the baking dish with boiling water until it reaches about halfway up the sides of the ramekins. Pop into the oven and cook for 35 minutes, or until the egg mixture is set but still has a slight wobble.

Remove the dish from the oven and leave to cool. Once the ramekins have cooled down, remove from the water and put into the fridge to cool completely. Sprinkle a teaspoon of caster sugar onto each crème brûlée and shake gently to cover the whole top.

Using a blowtorch, melt the sugar until liquid, then wait for it to harden into a crunchy top before serving. Alternatively, use a grill. Make sure it is really hot and place the crème brûlée as close to the grill as possible. Watch very closely to make sure the sugar doesn't burn. Serve.

NUTRITIONAL INFO PER SERVING

Mains	ENERGY KJ/KCAL	FAT (G)	SATURATED FAT (G)	CARBS (G)	SUGAR (G)	FIBRE (G)	PROTEIN (G)
BLT PASTA SALAD	1773/419	5.5	0.9	57	8.8	4.9	32
LOADED CURRY BURGER	1585/376	8.3	1.7	38	7.7	2.5	36
LASAGNE	1648/392	11	5	36	17	5.7	33
CHILLI BEAN SOUP	600/142	2.1	0.6	18	7.3	7.3	8.4
CARBONARA RISOTTO	1785/423	8.5	3.3	64	3.8	2.4	22
MUSHROOM AND SPINACH CURRY	700/167	6.4	0.6	17	6.5	4.2	8.7
COWBOY PIE	1908/453	9.1	3.3	61	16	12	25
CHICKEN FAJITA PASTA	2077/491	4.1	0.6	78	11	9	31
CREAMY PASTA WITH BACON, PEAS AND MUSHROOMS	2249/532	6.9	2.4	81	10	9.5	32
CHILLI MEATBALL ORZO	1501/356	6.8	2.3	40	9.3	9	28
COTTAGE PIE	1522/361	6.9	2.8	40	12	7.8	31
PESTO AND GREEN BEAN SPAGHETTI	888/210	3.3	1.6	34	2.6	3.5	9.1
FAJITA BOMBS	1594/379	11	5.8	31	7.4	5.1	37
SLOW-COOKER ALL-DAY BREAKFAST	1478/352	12	3.1	23	8.7	7.1	36
SPICY SAUSAGE AND TOMATO RICE	1702/402	3.9	1.4	70	10	4.5	19
FISH FINGER PIE	2061/490	13	4.2	64	6.5	9.7	25
VEGGIE QUESADILLAS	1264/302	10	4.3	34	8.7	9.1	13
HUNTER'S CHICKEN PASTA BAKE	1238/293	4.9	1.5	33	8.3	3.5	27
MUSHROOM MASALA	559/132	1.3	0.1	18	12	4.3	10
LEMON CHICKEN AND SPINACH PASTA	1135/269	5.2	2.2	27	2.1	2.4	27

Mains CONTINUED	ENERGY KJ/KCAL	FAT (G)	SATURATED FAT (G)	CARBS (G)	SUGAR (G)	FIBRE (G)	PROTEIN (G)
BOMBAY-STYLE POTATO AND CHICKEN TRAYBAKE	2304/546	9.5	2.3	46	15	8.5	64
MARMITE PASTA	1669/394	3.5	1	68	12	6.2	20
MEATBALL MASH BAKE	1747/414	8.9	4	43	13	7	36
MINCED BEEF HOTPOT	1759/417	7	2.9	51	10	8.9	33
CHICKEN TIKKA NACHOS	1510/359	12	2.4	42	13	4.6	19
SNEAKY MAC AND CHEESE	990/235	6.1	3.2	30	5.3	3.5	14
CHICKEN AND SPRING VEGETABLE ORZOTTO	1690/400	6	2	46	3.7	6	37
SALT AND PEPPER CHICKEN	1241/294	7.2	2	7.3	2.3	1.5	51
SAUSAGE-STUFFED PASTA SHELLS	1456/345	7.5	3.2	47	14	6.9	18
MAC AND CHEESE LASAGNE	1848/438	8.9	4	57	15	6.1	29
CHEESY PARSNIP SOUP	621/148	6	3.2	13	6.5	4.7	7.8
SAUSAGE TRAYBAKE	1538/365	7	2	54	31	8.8	17
CHICKEN AND CHIPS PIE	1348/320	6.4	2	30	5.4	4.3	43
GINGERED PORK	1198/285	9.6	3.1	21	12	3.9	27
TUNA AND TOMATO SPAGHETTI	1607/380	4.2	1.4	57	7.2	5.1	25
CHILLI MAC 'N' CHEESE	2221/528	13	6.2	57	17	11	38
SPAGHETTI BOLOGNESE	1809/428	5.9	2	63	12	7	26
HONEY SOY CHICKEN THIGHS	1437/341	8.3	2.2	15	14	0.5	51
CREAMY TARRAGON CHICKEN PASTA	1395/330	5.9	2.5	39	4.3	3.1	29
SPICY TOMATO SOUP	409/116	1.7	0	17	15	4.5	3.9

Mains CONTINUED	ENERGY KJ/KCAL	FAT (G)	SATURATED FAT (G)	CARBS (G)	SUGAR (G)	FIBRE (G)	PROTEIN (G)
ENCHILADA SLIDERS	1439/341	6.4	2.3	45	10	8.2	21
SPINACH AND PARMESAN ORZO	1067/253	4.9	2.2	39	4.9	3.5	12
VEGAN KATSU CURRY	1185/283	11	1.6	26	7.5	6.5	19
STICKY HARISSA AND ORANGE CHICKEN	1664/394	7.7	2.1	26	2.2	2.3	53
BAKED BEAN CHILLI	1189/282	4.8	1.7	31	19	11	23
CREAMY BEEF AND POTATO PIE	1381/327	6.4	2.8	37	13	6.4	26
CHICKEN, BACON AND LEEK SOUP	713/169	3	0.9	19	4.5	3.4	15
PINEAPPLE PORK	1615/387	20	7.1	26	17	4	26
ROASTED BUTTERNUT SQUASH PASTA	1333/316	5.8	2.9	48	10	5	15
TOMATO AND CARAMELIZED ONION TARTS	922/220	9.7	4.7	24	5.1	2.9	7
CURRIED MACARONI CHEESE	1811/430	11	5.9	56	13	5.6	23
BAKED TERIYAKI TOFU	812/194	7.1	1.1	19	5.4	4.2	15
KEEMA SPAGHETTI	1398/331	5.2	1.7	44	8.7	7.1	23
MIX-IT-UP MINCE	1358/323	8.1	3.2	27	19	7.5	32
CREAMY TOMATO PASTA BAKE	2071/490	7.1	2.9	77	21	8.8	23

Desserts	ENERGY KJ/KCAL	FAT (G)	SATURATED FAT (G)	CARBS (G)	SUGAR (G)	FIBRE (G)	PROTEIN (G)
BISCOFF BANANA BREAD	1098/262	12	3.8	33	10	1.3	5.7
NEAPOLITAN ICE POPS	355/84	1.8	1	14	12	1.7	1.4
APPLE FRITTERS	1021/207	2.9	0.6	39	21	3.6	4.8
ORANGE RICOTTA CAKE	574/138	8.2	3	15	0.8	0.8	4.3
CREAMY RASPBERRY SLICES	1381/308	13	6.4	37	5.8	4.5	13
LEMON CURD SWISS ROLL	533/126	2.9	0.8	23	9.8	0.5	4
APPLE CRUMBLE SQUARES	324/78	1.7	0.5	18	0.8	0.5	1.2
CAPPUCCINO LAVA CAKES	920/159	14	5.6	19	3.5	0.6	5.8
NORWEGIAN-STYLE APPLE CAKE	517/124	6.4	2.1	16	6.4	0.7	1.8
STRAWBERRY GALETTE	1356/326	20	9.4	29	5.6	5	4.8
LEMON MERINGUE POTS	1124/268	9.1	2.4	48	8.2	1.9	4.9
RASPBERRY COOKIE BROWNIES	538/129	6.8	2.4	14	1.7	1	4.3
EVE'S PUDDING	1511/271	18	5.9	50	19	2.5	4.8
HOT CHOCOLATE MICROWAVE MUG CAKES	1182/193	13	4.9	29	19	1.8	5.8
LEMON DRIZZLE SWIRLS	418/100	4.1	1.9	13	3.8	0.7	2.3
MALT CHOCOLATE ICE CREAM	992/235	5.3	3.1	42	31	2.3	3.8
PEANUT BUTTER AND CHOCOLATE MOUSSE	954/230	18	8.3	8.8	8.2	1	6.5
PINEAPPLE FRITTERS	1040/246	2.3	0.5	43	23	4.4	11
SPRINKLE SPONGE	431/71	5.8	1.9	12	4.5	0.5	1.5
WHITE CHOCOLATE AND ORANGE CRÈME BRÛLÉE	780/186	8.4	3.9	22	16	0.5	6.9

INDEX

Note: page numbers in **bold** refer to illustrations.

ACKNOWLEDGEMENTS

We owe many thank yous to many people who work so hard to bring this book together. Without these people, there would be no book. We deeply appreciate you all and can't thank you enough for the time and effort you put into making this book something we are immensely proud of.

We want to say a huge thank you, firstly, to all of our followers on social media and all those who continue to make our recipes and let us know what you want next! We're so proud that Pinch of Nom has helped, and continues to help, so many people.

Thank you to our publisher Carole Tonkinson. To Martha Burley, Bríd Enright, Jodie Mullish, Annie Rose, Sarah Badhan, Amy Winchester and the rest of the team at Bluebird for helping us create this book and continuing to believe in Pinch of Nom throughout our journey. Major thanks also to our agent Clare Hulton for your unwavering support and guidance.

To Ellis Parrinder for the amazing photos and to Kate Wesson and Octavia Squire for making our food look so, so good. Thanks also to Sophie Denmead and Kristine Jakobsson for all your assistance. Big thanks go out to Nikki Dupin and Beth Free at Nic & Lou for making this book so beautiful!

We also want to thank our friends and family who have made this book possible. A very big thank you to Dr Hannah Cowan, Helen Child Villiers, Katie McKenna, Nicola Brooks and Jayne Dawson. Your support has meant the world.

Special thanks go to Laura Davis and Katie Mitchell for the endless hours you've put into this and for working so hard to get things right!

A huge thank you to our wonderful team of recipe developers who work tirelessly to help us bring these recipes to life: Lisa Allinson, Sharon Fitzpatrick and Holly Levell.

Massive thanks also go to Sophie Fryer, Hannah Cutting, Nick Nicolaou, Ellie Drinkwater and Laura Valentine for your writing and marketing support. To Cate Meadows and Jacob Lathbury for your creative and visual genius.

Additional thanks to Matthew Maney, Jessica Molyneux, Rosie Sparrow, Rubi Bourne, Vince Bourne and Cheryl Lloyd for supporting us and the business – we are so proud to work alongside you all.

To our wonderful moderators and online support team; thank you for all your hard work keeping the peace and for all your support.

Furry thanks to Mildred, Wanda, Ginger Cat, Freda and Brandi for the daily moments of joy.

And finally ... Huge thanks go to Paul Allinson for your support and advice. And to Cath Allinson who is never forgotten. YNWA.

ABOUT THE AUTHORS

KATE and KAY

Founders of Pinch of Nom
www.pinchofnom.com

Kate and Kay Allinson owned a restaurant together on the Wirral, where Kate was head chef. Together they created the Pinch of Nom blog with the aim of teaching people how to cook. They began sharing healthy, slimming recipes and today Pinch of Nom is the UK's most visited food blog with an active and engaged online community of over 3 million followers.